THE INDIANS OF LOUISIANA

The Indians of Louisiana

by

FRED B. KNIFFEN

Professor of Geography and Anthropology
Louisiana State University

WITH ILLUSTRATIONS BY
MILDRED COMPTON

PELICAN PUBLISHING COMPANY
GRETNA 1985

FOREWORD TO THE 1965 EDITION

The Bureau of Educational Materials and Research in the College of Education at Louisiana State University is pleased to make available to the school children of Louisiana, classroom teachers, administrative and supervisory personnel, and the lay public a valuable publication entitled *The Indians of Louisiana*.

In the early 1940s Dr. E. B. Robert, then Dean of the College of Education, conceived the idea of utilizing noted authorities on the faculty of Louisiana State University to prepare teaching materials designed to meet the special needs of the schools of Louisiana.

The first edition of this book, prepared by Dr. Fred B. Kniffen, Professor of Geography and Anthropology at Louisiana State University, and Mrs. May W. DeBlieux, Editor in the Bureau, was released in 1945 as the second booklet in the University Social Studies Series. Since the initial printing, *The Indians of Louisiana* has been widely acclaimed as a significant classroom teaching material. The demand for additional copies has been continuous, despite the fact that the initial supply has long since been distributed.

Through the full cooperation of Mr. Ray Nolen, Manager of the Louisiana State University Bookstore, and Dr. Fred B. Kniffen, the author, it is now possible for the Bureau of Educational Materials and Research to release the second edition of *The Indians of Louisiana*. We are confident that the publication will continue to receive an enthusiastic welcome from teachers, students, and the lay public.

JOHN A. HUNTER, *President*
Louisiana State University

L. L. FULMER, *Dean*
College of Education
Louisiana State University

Editor's note: Dr. Hunter and Dr. Fulmer are now retired from LSU after many years of distinguished service.

CONTENTS

INTRODUCTION

Did you ever walk between the corn rows after a rain and come suddenly upon a perfect arrowhead? Have you seen a little hill with live oaks growing on it and been told that it was an Indian mound? Did you ever see a real Indian walking silently along the street in Houma, Charenton, Elton, or Jena? Have you wondered about the Indians, where they came from, how they lived, what became of them?

This little book tells about Louisiana's first people, the Indians; how they came to a new country and made it their home, many hundreds of years ago. It traces the changes that slowly took place as the Indians developed new ways. Finally, it records the coming to Louisiana of the white man, an event that meant the beginning of the end for the Indians.

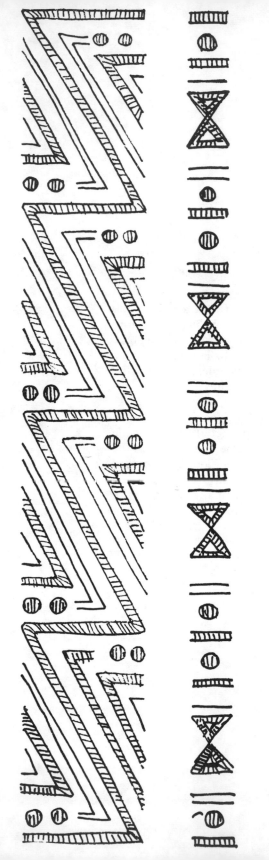

CHAPTER 1

STUDYING THE INDIANS

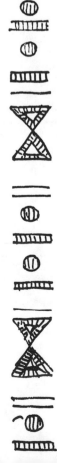

Ever since white men from Europe first saw the strange dark-skinned Indians in America, there have been persons who studied the Indians and wrote about them. At first most of the students and writers were preachers and priests or traders and soldiers. Now there are many people who do nothing but study the Indians. There are museums in most cities where you can see arrows, baskets, clothing, and many other things made by Indians. Hundreds of books have been written about them.

Students soon decided that the study of the Indians must be divided into two parts called prehistoric and historic. The prehistoric deals with the Indians during the long period of time before the coming of the white man. The historic begins with European settlements in America. For Louisiana, the historic part is the study of the Indians since Iberville and other white men began to settle our state in the year 1700.

The main reason for dividing the study of the Indians into prehistoric and historic parts is that one part must be studied in a different way from the other. Like most Indians, those of Louisiana had no writing and no books, so nothing was written about them until white men came here to live. We can read about the historic Indians, but the study of those who lived in prehistoric times is more difficult.

⊙ CONE ⊙⊙ SQUARE ⊙⊙ RECTANGLE ⊙〰⊙

READING THE ANCIENT RECORD

If it were your job to study the prehistoric Indians of Louisiana, how would you go about it? Remember that they left no writing, no books, and no calendars. Then what is there to study that will tell you about them?

First there are the Indian mounds. Mounds are most often made of earth but some of them are made of shells. Some mounds are round at the bottom and rise up to a rounded top or peak, so that they look like domes or cones. Other mounds are square or rectangular at the bottom and have flat tops, so that they look like pyramids whose peaks have been cut off. There is one mound that is different from any other in Louisiana. It lies on the shore of Grand Lake in Cameron Parish. This mound is made of clam shells, many, many thousands of them. But what is more important, it is shaped like an alligator, so much so that the Indians certainly built it to look like one. Part of the mound has been washed away by the lake. The part that is left is over 500 feet long and shows the body, tail, and three legs of the alligator.

Suppose that a lake or a river or a highway has cut into the side of a mound so that you can see what is inside. If you look carefully you may find arrowheads; whole clay pots or pieces of them; stone axes; animal bones; bones of human beings who were buried in the mound; mats made of split cane; and a whole great variety of things. All of these things belonged to the builders of the mound.

If the river or lake or highway hasn't cut the mound open for you, you can do it yourself. With a shovel or even with a team and plow you can tear the mound down and see what is inside. But, if you dig a mound that way, you will destroy forever a part of the record that is needed to get the story of the prehistoric Indians of Louisiana. No one should ever dig into a mound unless he has learned how to do it properly. You may sometime have a chance to see how an archaeologist works. An archaeologist is a person who has been trained to dig a mound in such a way that none of the record is lost. Just how does he go about it?

First he clears off the trees and brush. Then he drives stakes in the mound to form five-foot squares. Each stake has a number. A map is made showing the height and position of the stakes. Then it is time to start digging. There are several ways to dig, but the most common one starts with a straight trench or ditch that is deep enough to be below the bottom of the mound. This trench lies outside the mound but close to its edge. The diggers work from the side of the trench, toward and through the mound. The dirt is removed in slices, very much as one cuts a loaf of bread.

The heavy digging is done with shovels, but as soon as anything is found, it is carefully dug out with a small trowel and cleaned off with a whiskbroom. Skeletons and pottery are photographed and everything is measured from the stakes so that the archaeologist can tell later just what part of the mound it came from. The articles found are called specimens. Every single thing worth saving must have a number written on it, for it is easy to forget when there are thousands of articles to remember.

This plan of numbering is a good thing to keep in mind if you collect arrowheads. Let us suppose that you find six heads in one field. Put the same number on all

[11]

SHELL BEADS

MENDED POT

POTSHERDS

BONES

the heads and in a notebook write, for example, that you got six arrowheads numbered 14 from Jones' field on August 7, 1944. If you follow this plan, your collection can help the archaeologist when he is writing the history of the Indians.

After the archaeologist has finished digging a mound, he puts all the earth back so that the mound looks as it did before the digging started. All the specimens that have been found are carried away to the laboratory. There they are cleaned, the pots are mended, the photographs developed, and the field notes are written in the permanent record. Then the archaeologist is ready to study what he has found to see what it can tell him about the Indians. What he would like to know is the whole story of the people who built the mound—who they were, when and how they lived. All the questions can never be answered, but they form the goal toward which he works.

The archaeologist now spreads all the specimens out on a big table. What a collection it is! There are whole pots and also pieces of pots (called potsherds) ; beads and necklaces of shell; tools and weapons of stone, bone, and horn; human bones and bones of animals. Have you noticed that nothing has been said about clothing, blankets, baskets, bows, and shafts or handles for spears? Why not? It is because things made of cloth, skin, and wood don't last long when they are left outside in our warm, damp Louisiana climate. Articles made of stone, clay, and bone last for a much longer time, so they are the things that the archaeologist must work with. But now he is beginning his study. Let us join him as he examines the specimens spread out on the big table.

We shall suppose that this particular mound is a

very unusual one, one that was built bit by bit by different tribes during several hundreds of years. We look first at the things that came from the bottom of the mound, since the bottom must be the oldest part, the part that was built first. The pottery is very simple, rough and with little decoration. There are also charred human bones, showing that the older tribe burned the bodies of the dead. We examine tubes of baked clay that were used for smoking. Our record shows that we found a circle of post holes filled with dirt. This means that a round house was built.

The specimens from the top of the mound are quite different. The pottery is much better made, thin and smooth, with many rounding lines for decoration. The bones show that the dead were not burned but were buried sitting upright with their knees drawn up under their chins. There are pipes for smoking, but these pipes are clay bowls with holes at one side to put stems in. A square of post holes shows that a square house was built.

Now the archaeologist knows quite a great deal about the two prehistoric tribes that built the mound. The two tribes may be called the Old People and the New People. He finds other mounds in Louisiana that were built by the Old People and also more that were built by the New People. The pottery, the tools, weapons, and the burials all tell him whether it was Old People, New People, or some different people who built the mound he is studying. Our busy archaeologist digs in still other places and finds articles much like those used by the New People. In addition, he finds rusted iron axes, glass beads, and other things that were made by white men and traded to the Indians. He has discovered a new tribe that must have lived at the end of prehistoric times,

[13]

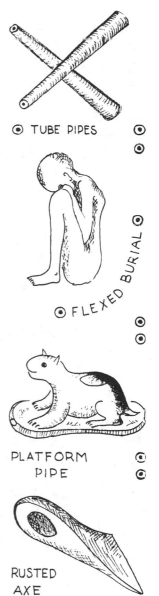

TUBE PIPES

FLEXED BURIAL

PLATFORM PIPE

RUSTED AXE

INDIAN MIDDEN

MODERN MIDDEN

that is, around 1700, and he names it Newer People. Digging in more mounds, the archaeologist finds proof of a tribe still older than the Old People. This tribe he calls the Older People. Now he knows of four prehistoric peoples. He could show them in an outline, with the oldest tribe at the bottom:

1700 . . . . Newer People
New People
Old People
Older People

The task of the archaeologist is much more difficult than it appears to be in the last few paragraphs. But now you know what he tries to do and something of the way in which he goes about it.

The archaeologist can dig in a midden as well as in a mound. In fact, a midden is in some ways a much better place to dig than a mound. But what is a midden? A midden is simply an old dump heap, made like our modern dump heaps of everything that is old or broken and has been thrown away. Middens are as big or bigger than mounds, but they don't look like mounds because they have no regular shape. They are made of black earth or of clam shells mixed with black earth.

Middens must be dug in the same careful way that mounds are. They have in them at least a little of everything that the Indians made or used. That is why they are often better places to dig than mounds. It may be that hundreds of years from now archaeologists will dig in our dump heaps to find out about things that we think aren't important enough to write about now.

Other places where the archaeologist can find tools, weapons, and pottery are fields where Indian villages

[14]

once stood. In the hilly parts of Louisiana, where the ground is covered with gravel, he may find old Indian workshops where stone arrow points, drills, and knives were made.

Even with all the digging and all the studying that has been done, there are many things about the prehistoric Indians that are not known. Probably we shall never learn many things that we should like to know about them. However, we do know the main parts of the story.

Words to explain and remember:

If you need help, turn to the key on page 107.

museum	(mū zē'ŭm)
historic	(hĭs tŏr'ĭk)
prehistoric	(prē'hĭs tŏr'ĭk)
rectangular	(rĕk tăng'ŭ làr)
pyramid	(pĭr'à mĭd)
archaeologist	(är kē ŏl'ô jĭst)
specimen	(spĕs'ĭ mĕn)
field notes	
charred	(chärd)
midden	(mĭd'ĕn)
laboratory	(lăb'ôr à tō rĭ)
permanent	(pûr'mà nĕnt)
potsherd	(pŏt'shûrd)
pottery	(pŏt'ēr ĭ)
Houma	(Hōō'mà or Hō'mà)
Charenton	(Chăr'ĕn tŏn)
Elton	(El'tŏn)
Jena	(Jē'nà)
Cameron Parish	(Kăm'ĕr ŏn)
Grand Lake	

[15]

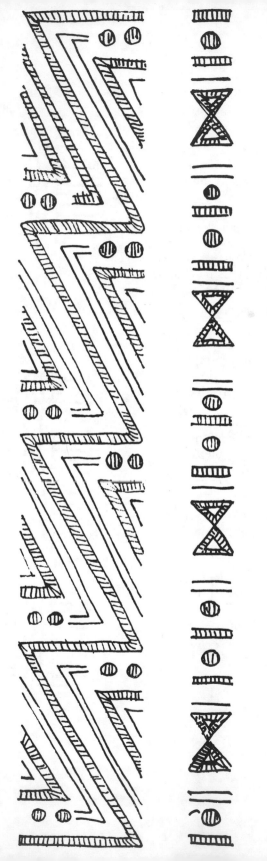

CHAPTER 2

THE FIRST INDIANS

COMING OF THE INDIANS TO AMERICA

Most people who study the Indians believe that they came from Asia. For one thing, the people who live in Asia look very much like Indians. Both have dark-brown skins and straight black hair. They look and are so much alike that they must have been one and the same people a long time ago. Since it is known that the people of Asia didn't go there from America, the Indians must have come here from Asia.

The first Indians to come to America didn't get on a big ship and sail across the Pacific Ocean, as Englishmen sailed across the Atlantic Ocean to New England and Virginia. It was 15 to 20,000 years ago, long, long before the time of Christ, when the Indians first came. There were no big ships in those days and there were no maps of America. Nobody lived in America; nobody had ever seen it or even heard of it. It had a great many wild animals and fish. There were large forests and broad stretches of grass; mountains and plains; rivers and lakes. The only thing missing was man. America was ready and waiting for its people.

The first Indians were hunters and fishermen who lived in the cold lands of northeastern Asia. A few of them wandered to East Cape in Siberia. (East Cape is the point on the coast of Asia that lies closest to Amer-

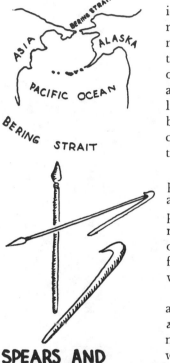

SPEARS AND
SPEAR THROWER

ican shores.) It is possible that one fine clear day the real discoverer of America climbed to the top of a hill near East Cape. Looking to the eastward, across the waters of Bering Strait, he saw the faint outline of the hills on Cape Prince of Wales in Alaska. In Bering Strait, about halfway between the two capes, he observed two little rocky islands. Then he hurried down the hill and brought the news to the other members of his tribe. Of course he didn't know that he had discovered a new continent. He didn't even know what a continent is.

Perhaps it wasn't long before some fisherman paddled his boat across the strait to Alaska. It is only about 35 miles across and the fisherman could have stopped at the islands, halfway over. Or, the first Indian to reach America may have been a hunter who walked across on the ice in winter. Whether hunter or fisherman, he found a land whose animals had never been hunted and whose waters had never been fished.

The first Indians were interested in better hunting and fishing, for it was not easy for them to get the food and skins that they needed in order to live. They knew nothing of farming, although they may have gathered wild berries, nuts, and roots. Of course they had no guns; they didn't even have bows and arrows. Their two most important weapons were the spear and the harpoon. The spear was thrown with the spear thrower which is a short stick with a hook on one end. The spear thrower was held with the throwing hand and the hook was fitted over the end of the spear handle. With this clever invention the hunter was able to throw his spear faster and farther.

The harpoon used by the early Indians looked somewhat like a spear, since both had pointed heads and

[18]

shafts. But there was an important difference: the head of the harpoon was tied to a long string. The other end of the string was held by the thrower. When the harpoon was thrown into an animal, the head slipped off and worked into the animal's body, carrying with it the string held by the hunter. When the animal was dead the hunter pulled it to him. Harpoons were used especially for fishing and for hunting animals that live in the water. The harpoon is such a good weapon that modern forms of it are still used by white men for hunting whales.

There were other simple weapons and tools: awls or punches of bone; knives of stone or bone; plain wooden drill sticks for making fire by twirling or turning fast between the hands; clubs of wood; horn tools for flaking or chipping flints. There were no iron or steel tools and weapons; the time of metals lay far in the future.

Everything these first Indians had was plain and simple. Their houses had only one room and were made of earth, skin, and wood. They covered their bodies as best they could with skins, since they had no real clothing. They must have been very cold sometimes, and no doubt during the cold northern winter they stayed in their houses a great deal. They had dogs but there were no horses, cows, pigs or other tame animals. There must have been times when food was very scarce.

It is not surprising that the Indians pushed southward toward warmer and better lands than Alaska. But they did not move rapidly. One family might move a few miles one year in search of better hunting and fishing. The next year another family would move a few miles farther. It took hundreds of years for the Indians

[19]

STONE AXE

to spread up the Yukon Valley to Canada and south through the Great Plains to the United States. (Of course there was no "Canada" and there was no "United States" then.) It took many hundreds of years more to get to Mexico and South America. Everywhere they went the pioneer Indians found a land without people. They found warm lands and cold lands; rainy lands and dry ones; forested lands and grasslands; good fishing and hunting and poor fishing and hunting. Onward and ever onward they pushed, a few at a time.

While the first Indians were spreading over the new country, more and more little groups of people were coming from Asia. The newer Indians looked a little different from the first ones and they probably spoke a different language. But what is far more important, they brought the bow and arrow with them and they knew how to grind hard stones to make stone axes.

After several thousand years there were at least a few Indians in nearly every part of the two Americas. Once they had settled in a new kind of country, they began to develop new ways to live. The Indians who settled in deserts learned how to find water and how to use the desert plants and animals. Those who settled near lakes invented new kinds of boats and learned new ways to catch fish. The Indians who lived in the high countries of Mexico and Peru developed farming. These same Indians learned how to build buildings of stone, and one tribe invented writing and made books. When new and better ways of doing things were found, the news slowly spread from one tribe to the next. It is not greatly different in our modern world, except that today the news of new inventions spreads much more rapidly.

[20]

The First Indians in Louisiana

The first Indians reached Louisiana about a thousand to two thousand years ago. That was many thousands of years after the Indians first came to America from Asia. If you had arrived with those first Louisiana Indians, you would not have recognized the country in which you live today. Remember that no people had ever lived in what is now Louisiana. There were no fields, no towns, no roads, no houses. There was only the land as nature had made it: wild animals and fish; great forests of pine and cypress; wide stretches of marsh, swamp, and prairie. There were no levees to keep the rivers from flooding. The streams were not in the same places as they are today. Even the Mississippi River was flowing along a different course.

Louisiana's first Indians seem to have been much like the first Indians to come to America from Asia. They had no bows and arrows and they made no pottery. They didn't even have stone axes and they knew nothing of raising crops. Then just how did they live? The easiest way to find out is to visit one of the Indian villages. Of course we can't really do it, but let's imagine that we can. We had better be invisible so that the Indians cannot see us and will not be afraid of us.

The Midden Village

It is a clear day in the marshes of south Louisiana. The wind is blowing enough to bend the tall grass before it and to roughen the water of the big lake until it sparkles in the sun. Away on the opposite shore is what looks like an island or hill rising above marsh and water. It is white at the bottom but the top is a mass of green. As we come closer, we see that the island is what we

[21]

PRAIRIE

MARSH

PINE FOREST

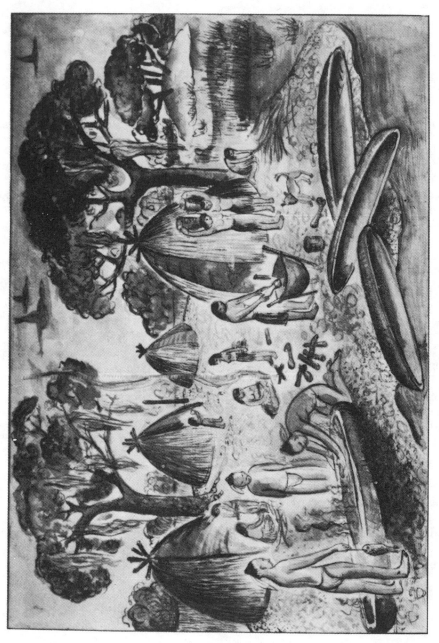

A MIDDEN VILLAGE

would call a midden. It is a great heap of white clam shells and dirt. The green near its top is the leaves of live oak trees growing there.

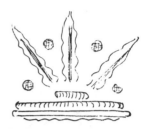

But there is something more than trees on the midden. There are people. They have no shoes or moccasins and they wear very little clothing. We can tell from their brown skins and the shape of their faces that they are Indians. The first person we notice is an old man who is scraping charcoal out of one end of a cypress log. A fire is burning slowly in the center of the log. Drawn up on the edge of the shells just beyond are three little boats or pirogues. We realize that the old man is making a pirogue by burning out a log.

On top of the midden are four little round houses and a new house is being built. We watch the men stick poles in the ground and bend them over to tie them to poles on the opposite sides. When the framework is completed, it is covered with palmettos.

STONE BOILING

There are baskets but no pottery. Near the fire is a deerskin, its edges held up by stakes so that it sags in the center to make a pocket that is filled with water and deer meat. An old woman sits by the fire. Now and then she reaches into the coals with a pair of tongs made of a doubled green branch. She plucks out a hot clay ball that makes the water sizzle as she drops it into the skin pocket. The water gets hotter and hotter until finally the meat is cooked. This way of cooking is called stone boiling. Until the Indians learned to make pottery, stone boiling was the only way they had of cooking anything in water.

We leave the old woman to see why the dogs are growling and fighting. They run away when we come close and we find that they have been quarreling over scraps on the garbage pile. We see the bones of deer, rac-

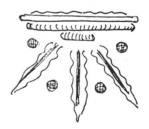

[23]

coons, opossums, muskrats, turtles, and some of other animals that we can't name. We notice a few fish bones too. It looks as if the Indians have plenty of meat to eat. We may think that meat and a few fish are all they have to eat until we remember that the whole midden hill is made of clam shells and that the Indians have eaten all the clams that lived in those shells. Then we wonder if the Indians don't get a little tired of clams once in a while.

CLAM

It would seem that life on the midden is a busy one. The women are cooking, tanning skins, or weaving baskets. During the heat of the day the men squat in the shade of the oaks. As they sit there, they are working. One is making awls from pieces of bone. They will be used for punching holes in leather. Another man breaks, cuts, and grinds bone and horn to make spear and harpoon points. When the late afternoon brings coolness, the men will paddle away in their pirogues, some to hunt, others to fish or to gather clams.

As we leave the little midden village and return to the present, perhaps we think that we might like to have lived in those olden days. How good it seems: no war; no money; no school; hunting and fishing all the time. But then, there were also no radios, no motion pictures, no books, no ice cream, no warm houses, no doctors. Would we care to trade?

Words to explain and remember:

harpoon	(här poon′)
spear thrower	
invention	(ĭn věn′shŭn)
flaking	(flāk′ĭng)
fire drill	

[24]

pirogue   (pē'rōg)
palmettos   (păl mĕt'tōz)
awls   (ôlz)
Siberia   (Sī bēr'ĭ à)
Yukon Valley   (Yū'kŏn)
Peru   (Pḕ rōō')

CLAM.

CLAM

MARKSVILLE BURIAL MOUND

CHAPTER 3
THE MOUND BUILDERS

The years come and go and our friends of the midden village are dead and buried deep in the shell heap. Their great-grandchildren are now men and women. If we could visit the village again we would not think at first that there had been any changes. But if we looked closely and remembered exactly what we had seen before, we would realize that two new and very important things had been added: pottery, and bows and arrows.

From the people who lived to the north or west, the Louisiana Indians had learned how to coil rods of clay to make pots, how to smooth them, and how to bake them in fire so they would hold water. How much easier it was to set a pot over the fire than to cook by stone boiling! From the same people the first bow and arrow were brought to Louisiana. The bow was a great improvement over the spear, for it meant easier and better hunting.

Even with pottery and the bow, life was not changed much. Perhaps the Indians ate fewer clams and more meat; probably they didn't have to work quite so hard; but their great-grandparents would still have felt at home in the midden village.

It was about 1,200 years ago when there began some truly great changes for Louisiana's Indians. New ideas and even some new people reached Louisiana from the west, having come probably from Mexico. So great were the changes that the new villages didn't look much like

[27]

ROUND COIL OF CLAY

SMOOTHING

SLIP DECORATION

MAKING POTTERY

the old ones, and they no longer had to be built near places where the Indians could get clams. What were the new ideas and new ways that could have such important effects?

One of them was a knowledge of farming, that is, planting and growing crops, especially corn. Raising corn didn't mean that Indians quit hunting and fishing—not a bit of it. It did mean that towns could be built away from the marshes, away from the lakes and bays where clams lived. It was often necessary to move to places where there was good soil for raising crops. Most of the Indians left the coastal part of Louisiana. They no longer had to live near the coast. Up the rivers and bayous they went to find high ground along the streams where the trees and brush could be cleared to make fields.

Another of the new ideas was to build cone-shaped mounds over the bones of dead people. You may have heard at some time that Indians built the mounds to live on when the ground was covered by flood water. This is certainly not true. There were floods in the olden days before levees, but as soon as the rivers flowed gently over their banks the water drained quickly to the swamps. The Indians learned all about floods, of course, so they always cleared their fields and built their houses and mounds on high ground.

Burial mounds were made of earth. The dirt was dug with sharp sticks from banks and carried in baskets to the place where the mound was to be built. A low earth platform was made first. On it were placed the bones of the dead, after they had been cleaned of flesh and sometimes burned a little. Usually a few small tools or weapons were broken and placed by the bones. Then more earth was brought to cover the skeletons and to

[28]

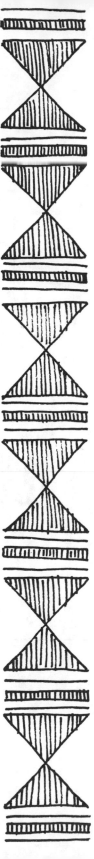

build the mound up to a peak. The early Indians must have had a great deal of respect for the mounds where their people were buried, for they always built their villages some distance away from them.

Farming and a special way to bury the dead weren't the only new ideas of the mound builders. They made and smoked clay pipes; they ground pieces of hard rock into stone axes; their pottery was much finer than any made before in Louisiana.

The first pipes were straight tubes of baked clay. One end of the tube had a large opening to hold the burning tobacco. At the other end was a small opening to draw the smoke through. It isn't known just what the Indians smoked at first. They may have raised tobacco in their gardens or perhaps they smoked wild tobacco or the bark and leaves of other plants.

The new stone axe wasn't as good as our modern steel axe, but it was certainly better than no axe at all. It took a long time to make a stone axe. The Indian had only one way to do it: he ground one stone down by rubbing it on another stone until he got the size and shape he wanted. Most stone axes of Louisiana Indians were made of a hard rock that is found nowhere in our state. This means that over a thousand years ago the Indians of Louisiana were trading with other Indians who lived at least as far away as Arkansas.

The Indian knew other ways of working in stone. One of the most surprising to us is the manner in which he drilled holes through pieces of solid rock. There were two ways to do it. One method was to use a stone drill that looks very much like a thin, sharp arrow point. It was fastened to a stick or shaft that was turned hour after hour between the palms of the hands until a hole was

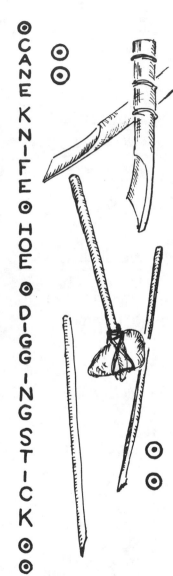

CANE KNIFE ⊙ HOE ⊙ DIGGING STICK

worn through the hard rock. For the other way to drill, the Indian used a hollow cane or reed. This he turned between his palms as described before. How could a soft cane or reed ever cut through rock? The secret is this: at the end of the cane that was turning against the rock were sand and water. The sand was kept moving by the turning drill and it was the sand that did the cutting.

Every Indian man made his own stone axe, just as he made every other weapon or tool that he used. His knives were pieces of flint or split canes with sharp edges. Hoes had blades of stone or bone bound to wooden handles. A shovel was only a sharpened stick. Fire was made by turning a wooden drill against a block of wood. Every woman could do all the things that women were supposed to do. There were no stores and there were no servants. Each Indian had to make things for himself or do without them.

The addition of new ways did not mean that old ways were forgotten. We haven't stopped the use of horses just because we have automobiles and tractors. The Indian kept on using spears and harpoons after he learned to use the bow and arrow. Clams were still good to eat after the Indian got corn. Then too, there were always persons who wanted to do things the old way as well as those who wanted to do them the new way, just as there are today.

The Marksville People

Other important changes came to Louisiana about a thousand years ago. More people drifted in from the west bringing ideas and customs that may have started in Mexico. There must have been travel up and down the Mississippi Valley, for pieces of copper from far-away

[30]

Lake Superior began to appear in Louisiana. Most of the Indians lived in a number of villages scattered through the central part of the state. One of their largest villages was located near the present town of Marksville in Avoyelles Parish. Because we know more about this village than we do about any other, we call all the Indians who lived in Louisiana at this time, "Marksville" people.

Let us visit a Marksville village to see how it compares with the midden village that we visited a thousand years before. We'll spend a day with Alla, a Marksville boy.

ALLA, A MARKSVILLE BOY

Alla awoke late on the day of our visit. His mother had let him sleep because there had been guests in the village the night before and Alla had stayed up long after his usual bedtime. He stretched lazily and glanced at the mat beds lining the walls of the little room. They were all empty except his own. He dropped back on his bed to think of the strange visitors.

They had arrived about sunset in two big pirogues. Their strange dress and strange speech meant that they were from the north. The goods in their boats showed that they were traders. After a meal of corn and meat, the visitors had brought out their wares: pieces of copper; crystals of glassy quartz; little cubes that looked like lead (galena) ; chunks of a hard, dark rock; thin, flat pieces of black rock (shale) ; heavy, dark-red pebbles (iron ore) . Alla didn't know it, but all the traders' goods had come from distant places. Lake Superior Indians had mined the copper and traded it to the tribe living next to them. The second tribe had traded the copper to a third, and so on down the Mississippi Valley until it

[31]

BEADS◦EAR PLUGS◦

CLAY BEADS

EAR PLUGS

reached Alla's village. It was the same with the other rocks that the traders brought, except that they had come from different places: Arkansas, Missouri, and Tennessee.

Although Alla didn't know where the pieces of stone had come from, he did know how they were to be used. The copper and galena could be pounded, drilled, and ground to make beads. Other pieces of copper would make fancy ear plugs. The hard, dark rock was to be ground into axes. The one lucky enough to get a quartz crystal would drill a hole through it and hang it on a string around his neck. The shale could be carved into little figures. The heavy iron ore was for plumb bobs or sinkers.

As Alla lay thinking of all these wonderful things, suddenly he realized he was hungry. Up he jumped and stepped out through the door into the bright sunshine. There was no dressing to do, for during the warm season Marksville boys wore nothing but a short apron, day and night.

Alla was blinded for a moment as he came out of the dark house. Soon he could see the fire and over it a pot partly filled with the corn and meat that he liked so well. He scooped out a bowlful of the warm food and began to eat greedily. First he drank a little of the soup, and then, with his fingers, he stuffed the solid parts into his mouth.

His hunger satisfied, Alla looked around and began to plan for the day. From where he stood, he could see all the village's 20 houses. All of them were square or rectangular in shape and were set partly into the ground, that is, the houses had been built over shallow holes dug into the earth. They had no windows; there were only

[32]

low doors through which one stepped down to the dirt floors. Alla didn't think it queer that there was no street and that every house pointed in a different direction.

He walked slowly around to the shady side of the house. There he found his mother, sister, and baby brother. Alla's mother was busy making pottery while his sister tended the baby. You certainly would have thought that a very mean trick was being played upon the helpless infant. A board was bound tightly against his forehead. It must have hurt, for he was crying and his sister couldn't make him stop. Alla saw nothing strange in what was being done to his brother. He thought that it was right to flatten foreheads. Hadn't his own been flattened when he was a baby?

There was nothing in the scene to interest Alla. He glanced to the west where he could see the tall corn in the gardens. He thought he had better sneak quietly and quickly away before his mother told him to find the hoe and get to work. His father and older brothers had gone on a trip to get arrowhead stones and salt. Their absence left Alla the only "man" at home. He was expected to do the men's work, but he didn't feel like working on this fine day.

Alla came back to the front of the house and walked on until he reached the high bank above the river. There he turned northward, away from the village. After going about a quarter of a mile, he came to a ditch and beyond it an earth wall. He scrambled across the ditch and up to the top of the wall. There he stopped because he was afraid to go any farther. Looking through the trees and brush inside the wall, Alla could see the tops of the mounds that covered the dead. Like many a white boy, he was afraid to go into a cemetery alone. Only twice had

HEAD FLATTENING

[33]

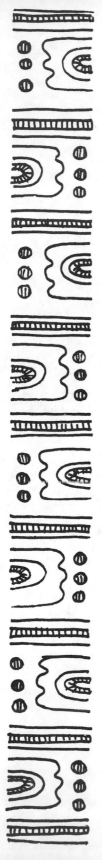

he been inside the wall and both times he had gone with the whole village.

A burial was the occasion for the first trip. While the women and children carried baskets of earth, the men built a rough box of logs on top of a large mound. The dirt was piled in an even slope from the ground to the top edge of the box. Then the hole made by the box was lined with cane mats and on its flat bottom were laid the bones of the dead. More mats were put over the bones and the box was closed with a lid made of heavy poles. Earth was heaped over the top until the mound was built up to a sharp peak. During the whole burial there had been sad singing, then periods of silence. Alla did not enjoy it at all. He was very glad when he could return to the village.

The second trip inside the wall was even worse than the first. Only a year ago bad Indians had come up the river from the south to steal and kill. News of the attack spread rapidly through the village. "Hurry inside the wall for protection from our enemies," was the word brought by the messenger. Everyone ran as fast as he could. The men were armed with clubs and bows. The women helped the children and snatched up what food they could carry. Alla went with the women and children to hide in the brush inside the wall. The men waited outside for the attackers. There was a short, fierce fight. Two of the enemy were killed, and their heads were cut off after the others had fled. There was a big victory dance while the heads were being buried in a mound. Poor Alla did not like the fight any more than he had liked the burial.

It made Alla uneasy to sit alone on the wall within sight of the burial mounds and the place where the battle

[34]

had been fought. Perhaps he had better go back to the village, even if he did have to work in the garden. But he needn't have worried about working, for just as he got to the first house he saw his father and brothers approaching from the west. Everything else was forgotten as the whole family gathered around the fire while the men smoked their long pipes and told of a successful trip.

Alla was most interested to hear about getting stone. His father told how they had walked for three days until they came to a place where a little river had cut through a whole bed of gravel. While the brothers hunted for big pieces of stone, Alla's father broke the rounded chunks into flat flakes with his heavy stone hammer. The flakes were made square or rectangular by trimming the rough edges. Then they were ready to be carried home where they would be chipped into arrowheads, knives, spearheads, and drills, when there was time to work on them.

When his father stopped talking Alla asked, "When will I be big enough to go on a trip with you?"

His father answered: "You are already big enough, but you can't go until you are brave and until you will do what you are supposed to do without being told."

Alla hung his head and wondered how his father knew that he was afraid at the wall and that he had neglected his work in the garden. He then and there made up his mind that he would do his work and that he would not be afraid. "Father will ask me to go with him on his next trip," Alla said to himself.

As we leave Alla and his village, we wonder why the Marksville people flattened their foreheads and buried their dead in mounds. Very strange customs, we think. But we should know that different peoples think and act

[35]

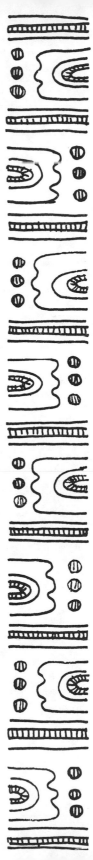

differently at different times, and the ways of one people may be just as right as those of another. It is a sign of ignorance to laugh at a person and to feel superior to him just because his ways seem strange.

Words to explain and remember:

coastal	(kōs'tǎl)
quartz	(kwôrtz)
galena	(gà lē'nǎ)
shale	(shāl)
earplugs	(ēr'plŭgz)
plumbbob	(plŭm'bŏb)
infant	(ĭn'fǎnt)
burial	(bĕr'ĭ ǎl)
protection	(prŏ tĕk'shŭn)
occasion	(ŏkā'zhŭn)
battleground	
Marksville	(Märks'vĭl)
Avoyelles Parish	(À voi'yĕlz)
Alla	(Ăl'à)

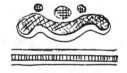

CHAPTER 4
The Last Mound Builders

The Temple Mounds

About 800 years ago there came to Louisiana's Indians some final great changes that lasted until the coming of white men to our state. These changes were brought from the west by people who flattened their foreheads just as the Marksville Indians had done.

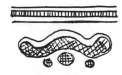

The most important change was a new kind of mound and the customs that went with it. Unlike the old cone-shaped burial mounds, the new mounds were flat-topped pyramids. Upon the flat tops were built round temples or churches. In the middle of each temple a pit or hole was dug in the ground. A fire was kept burning in the pit all the time. Every few years the temple was torn down, more earth was put on top of the mound, and then a new temple was built. The new temple mounds were high and steep, so the Indians built stairs of earth up one side.

Like burial mounds, temple mounds were generally built in groups, that is, several in one place. Two of the mounds were almost always placed so as to face each other across a square or plaza. The square was a meeting place for ceremonies or celebrations and worship. At Jonesville in Catahoula Parish there are the remains of a great group of temple mounds surrounded by a wall and ditch.

[37]

The first temple mounds were always located some distance away from any single village but close enough to several villages so that all the Indians could come together for ceremonies. Temple mounds were not used for burials. Some persons were buried in old-fashioned burial mounds. The graves of others were so well hidden that we haven't found them yet.

Early temple mounds are found along most of the bigger bayous and rivers of Louisiana, from the southern marshes north to Arkansas. So many mounds mean many Indians to build them. There seem to have been more Indians in Louisiana at this time than at any other period. Great numbers of clams were being eaten again and the empty shells piled into big middens. There were large fields of corn and other vegetables. A new, fine, red pottery was made. There do not seem to have been important wars. There were no epidemics of disease, with many people ill at once. It was surely a golden time, perhaps *the* golden time of Louisiana Indians!

Good times never last forever or there wouldn't be good times and bad times. After you reach the top of a hill, you can only go down on the other side. This is the way it was with Louisiana's Indians. The early Temple Mound people reached the top of the hill. Next came a flat stretch with little change and after that the descent down the other side of the hill. The changes came slowly at first, then faster and faster, until finally in our own time, the Indians have nearly disappeared.

Not every change was a bad one. The pottery became very good, probably the finest ever made by Louisiana Indians. There were many graves filled with beautiful pottery, tools, and weapons. However, there were

[38]

fewer new mounds. It was the first sign of going down hill. The Indians were becoming less in number. We know that they were restless, afraid, and angry. Strange and terrible dangers came to frighten the mound builders.

Because they were afraid, whole villages fled from the broad valleys of the big rivers to small valleys hidden away in the hills. The coast and the clam middens were almost entirely deserted. Houses were built close to the temple and burial mounds and to each other. Villages were protected by walls called stockades, made by sticking tall sharpened posts into the ground.

Running away and building strong towns couldn't halt what was happening to the Indians. Walls could not protect them from strange new diseases. The Indians died in large numbers. There were angry disputes and wars between villages that had always been friendly, which meant more deaths. Indeed it was a time of fear and sorrow.

Wars and fighting the Indians knew. They couldn't understand and they couldn't conquer new kinds of sickness. Neither the medicine men nor the gods that the Indians had believed in were able to help them. So a new religion and new gods were tried. In their ceremonies the Indians wore masks and charms, and had a special dress. By these means they hoped to drive evil away and bring back the good old days.

We wonder what caused all the trouble. What were the new diseases and where did they come from? Why was there war where there had been no war before? To answer these questions we must know that the unhappy times began about 1550.

Remember that Columbus reached America in 1492

[39]

MASKS AND CHARMS

A STOCKADE VILLAGE

and that DeSoto and his men were in Louisiana a few years before 1550. Europeans brought serious diseases like smallpox, and light diseases such as chicken pox and measles. All were new and serious to the Indians. Sometimes whole villages were wiped out by measles alone.

The Indians didn't know at first that the strange sickness came from white men. They thought that it came from the next village. They must have revenge on the wicked neighbors who had brought illness and death. It was lack of understanding that made enemies out of friends and brought more death and sorrow through war.

Thus it was that even before white people began to settle in Louisiana, the Indians were changing their ways and losing their hold on the land that had always been theirs. The power of the Europeans was pushing on ahead of the settlers themselves, who brought an end to prehistoric times.

The End of Prehistoric Times

It was about the year 1700 that white settlers came to Louisiana. Think how important it was for the Indians to live so near to white people that they could talk to them and see how they lived! Now the changes came faster and faster. More and more the Indians gave up their own ways of living and borrowed the ways of the white man.

For the one who studies the Indians, 1700 is an important date because it separates prehistoric from historic times. All we know about the prehistoric Indians we must get by digging in mounds and middens. What we know about the historic Indians we get only partly by digging in their old villages. For most of their history, we must read what some white man wrote about them a

[41]

long time ago. We can also find out a few things by talking with Indians who are living today. It is much easier to find out how people live by asking or watching them than it is by studying what they have thrown away or have buried in the ground. It is as though you were told to find out everything that a dog does for a whole day. It would be easy if you could follow him and see what he does. It would be very difficult if you waited until the next day, then tried to trace his tracks and guess what he had done.

OUTLINE OF THE PREHISTORIC INDIANS

Before we say goodbye to the archaeologist and leave the prehistoric Indians, let us make an outline of the main things that we have found out about prehistoric times in Louisiana. We must start with the oldest Indians, telling when and how they lived. Then we shall take up the Indians who came next, showing what new ways of living they added. The oldest tribe must be shown at the bottom of the outline, just as the oldest part of a mound or midden is at the bottom.

[42]

The Prehistoric Indians of Louisiana

1700—The end of the prehistoric and the beginning of the historic Indians

                    Late
                        Added: stockaded villages
                                greater interest in religion

Temple Mounds
                    Early
                        Added: temple mounds
                                red pottery

800 yrs. ago..
                    Marksville people
                        Added: metals
                                copper
                                galena
                                quartz crystals
                                walls and ditches around
                                    mounds

Burial Mounds

                    Early
                        Added: burial mounds
                                farming
                                tube pipes
                                stone axes

1200 yrs. ago...
                    Late
                        Added: pottery
                                bows and arrows

Middens
                    Earliest
                        Had: spears and throwers
                                harpoons
                                dogs
                                stone boiling

2000 (?) yrs. ago.....................................

Words to explain and remember:

plaza	(plä′zȧ)
ceremonies	(sĕr′ĕ̇ mŏn ēz)
worship	(wûr′shĭp)
epidemic	(ĕp ĭ dĕm′ĭk)
stockade	(stŏk ād′)
quartz crystals	(krĭs′ tȧlz)
Catahoula Parish	(Kăt ȧ hōō′lȧ)

CHAPTER 5

THE HISTORIC INDIANS

We have learned that the Indians described as historic are those who have been in touch with white people. This means that historic Indian time begins earlier in those parts of America first seen by white men. It comes later in distant places that were hard to reach. Historic time begins in Cuba about 200 years before it begins in Louisiana. Spaniards reached Cuba before 1500 and Frenchmen didn't begin to settle Louisiana until about 1700. Some parts of western and northern America were discovered much later than Louisiana was, so historic time in those places begins after 1700.

Thus for over 200 years after the arrival of Columbus, Europeans knew little about the Indians of Louisiana. However, they had learned a good deal about the other Indians of America.

NAMING THE INDIANS

Columbus named the Indians but he wasn't the first person from Europe to see America. Norsemen or Vikings had sailed along the coast of Labrador nearly 500 years before, in the year 1000. The Norsemen found a strange people living in the new land, a people that we now call Eskimos. But the discovery by the Norsemen was not very important because very few people in the world knew about it.

When Columbus landed on the island of San Sal-

[45]

SIGN LANGUAGE

ANTELOPE

HOUSE

BEAR

vador in 1492, he thought that he had arrived at the East Indies. That is why he gave the name "Indians" to the people who were living there. In a few years explorers found that two great continents, North and South America, blocked the way from Europe to Asia, sailing west. Thus Columbus had discovered new lands that weren't a part of the Indies at all, so their people shouldn't have been called Indians. But it was too late to change the name and Indian it has been ever since. Sometimes we say American Indians or Amerinds, to avoid confusing them with the Indians of India, a large country in Asia.

Different Kinds of American Indians

A stream of Europeans followed Columbus. They traveled widely over the new lands, finding out more and more about the Indians. All Indians, they found, looked very much alike, with their brown skins, coarse black hair, and dark eyes. But one tribe was not like every other tribe in the way it lived and acted.

The Spaniards found Indian tribes in Mexico and Peru who knew as much and lived as well as many people in Europe. Farming was far more important than hunting and fishing. There were big cities, stone buildings, paved roads, and bridges. Metals were dug out of mines and made into tools, weapons, and jewelry. Some knew how to read and write, and had books and libraries.

Englishmen in New England and Virginia found Indians who were very different from those of Mexico and Peru. Farming was no more important than hunting and fishing. There were no reading and writing, no use of metals. Houses were simple huts built of bark and skins.

[46]

Frenchmen on the St. Lawrence River in Canada met Indians who were even less advanced than those of New England and Virginia. Most Canadian Indians lived by hunting and fishing and planted no crops at all. But they gathered and cooked wild rice, and they got sap from maple trees to make sugar. They made boxes and canoes of birch bark and they used the bark to cover the wigwams they lived in.

One tribe, then, differed from another in many ways. There were various kinds of weapons and tools. Most Indians had never even heard of moccasins or buck-skin pants and shirts. The boats used in one place didn't look at all like those used elsewhere. Nearly every tribe had its own gods and its own religion.

Another difference is very important to the person who is studying the Indians: they spoke almost as many languages as all the rest of the world put together. Think of it! Very often the Indians of one tribe couldn't under-stand a single word spoken by the tribe living next to them. What could they do to be able to talk to each other? Well, members of one tribe could learn the lan-guage of the other tribe, or members of both tribes could learn to speak a language that didn't belong to either of them. Have you ever heard of the Indian sign language? It is one in which all the talking is done by making signs with the hands. It was invented by the tribes who hunted buffalo on the plains. The plains Indians spoke so many different languages that they had to have some way to understand each other.

Several languages were spoken by the Indian tribes of Louisiana. In order to talk to one another, a few mem-bers of each tribe learned the Mobilian language, which

[47]

ANTELOPE

HOUSE

BEAR

was the speech of the Indians who lived near Mobile in Alabama. Certain persons from two tribes talked to each other in Mobilian. Then in their own language they told the other members of their tribe what was being said.

So you see that all Indians didn't do things alike, they didn't think alike, and they didn't speak the same language. When someone who knows that you are studying the Indians asks you how the Indians did this or that, you should reply: "What Indian tribe do you mean? They weren't all alike, you know."

Things We Got From the Indians

FRUITS AND VEGTABLES

Most of the early Europeans thought that the Indians were poor, ignorant people who couldn't teach them anything. Many white Americans still think so. They should have to live for a few days without the things that the Indians gave us. Do you think that they would feel any loss? You probably know that pirogues, canoes, toboggans, snowshoes, and moccasins are used by many white Americans. But most of us could get along very easily without these gifts from the Indians. The most important things that we got from them are plants that they learned to use long before white men discovered America. Not one of them was used in other parts of the world before the time of Columbus. A list of all the plants given us by the Indians would fill a page. Here are a few of them: Irish and sweet potatoes; corn; tobacco; beans; squash; tomatoes; chocolate; pineapples; peanuts; tapioca (for tapioca pudding) ; quinine (for malaria) ; rubber; cotton. How different our lives would be without them! It makes us wonder what plants the Europeans used before they came to America.

[48]

The Arrival of the White Man in Louisiana

Until about 1700, Louisiana belonged to the Indians. They could live where they wanted to. They had to live in their own way. When Iberville and Bienville, the great French leaders, began to build forts and towns, it meant great changes for the Indians. The Frenchmen thought that Louisiana was their country, to be used just as they liked. The Indians didn't know at first that the white man claimed their country, but they did know very soon that he had many things which they would like to have. He had guns; steel knives, needles, and axes; glass beads; and copper kettles. The Indians wanted these and many other white man's articles because they were so much better than their own tools, weapons, and utensils. The more the Indians borrowed from the white man, the less they lived as they had before.

INDIAN POT

COPPER KETTLE

White people wanted a few things from the Indians: game and fish, skins and baskets. But getting these things didn't change the white people's ways of living very much. They thought that the Indians should live more like themselves, and especially that they should become Christians.

So, since the Indians were willing to change and the white men wanted them to, it is not surprising that the changes came rapidly. Fortunately for our study of the Indians, some of the early white men wrote about them before they had lost many of their old ways. Many of the writings are not very good and often they do not agree with each other. But they are the only record that we have. From these written records, and with a little help from modern Indians, we know a good deal about the

[49]

Indians of Louisiana as they were when white men first saw them.

Words to explain and remember:

toboggans	(tō bŏg'ănz)
snowshoes	
tapioca	(tăp ĭ ō' kȧ)
quinine	(kwī'nīn)
articles	
utensils	(ū tĕn'sĭlz)
Cuba	(Kū'bȧ)
Norsemen	(Nôrs'mĕn)
Vikings	(Vī'kĭngz)
San Salvador	(Sän Säl'vȧ dōr)
East Indies	
Amerinds	(Ăm'ēr ĭndz)
Mobilian	(Mō bēl' yăn)
Labrador	(Lăb'rȧ dôr)

CHAPTER 6
Louisiana Indian Tribes in 1700

In learning about the Indians of Louisiana, we shall need to know the answers to such questions as these: Who were the different tribes? Where did they live? How did they live?

It will be easier to understand who and where the Indian tribes were if you will study carefully the map on page 52 and the table on page 108. You will find that Louisiana is divided into six parts: Caddo, Tunica, Natchez, Atakapa, Chitimacha, and Muskogee. Some of these words you've heard before. You may know that one is the name of a city, another the name of a parish, and still another the name of some hills in West Feliciana Parish.

Sometimes we speak of the Caddo tribe or the Atakapa tribe, but that isn't quite right These names were selected by students of the Indians to divide Louisiana into the six different kinds of language that were spoken by its Indians. Each kind of language was spoken by one or more tribes, as you can see in the table. A tribe is a village or several villages of people having a single head chief. The members of one tribe may even join together to fight another tribe that speaks the same language. We may think of a tribe as an independent nation.

It is not known just how many Indian tribes lived in Louisiana, but certainly there was a large number.

[51]

INDIAN TRIBES
OF LOUISIANA
IN 1700

▲ Indian Villages
⌐┐ Language Areas
⌐┘
•MONROE Towns (modern)

CADDO

•KADOHADACHO

•SHREVEPORT

•YATASI   WASHITA▲

▲DOUSTIONY

NATCHITOCHES
ADAI▲▲

RED RIVER

MONROE•

TUNICA

▲KOROA

NATCHEZ

TENSAS▲

•NATCHEZ

ALEXANDRIA▲▲

▲AVOYEL

MARKSVILLE•

ATAKAPA

•OPELOUSA

CALCASIU R.

•LAKE
CHARLES

VERMILION R.

•ABBEVILLE

GRAND
LAKE

FRANKLIN•

BAYOU TECHE

HOUMA▲

MUSKHOGEE

OKELOUSA▲ •BATON ROUGE

TANGIPAHOA▲

▲ACOLAPISSA

BAYOUGOULA▲

PONTCHARTRAIN

QUINIPISSA ▲TANGUAHO

▲WASHA

CHITIMACHA

CHAWASHA
•HOUMA

BAYOU

LA FOURCHE

0 10 20   40   60
SCALE OF MILES

There were probably more than those shown in the table, and some that are in the table may not be right. We are not sure just what the truth is because the early writers didn't agree. In some cases they used the same names for different tribes and at other times they used different names for the same tribes. Isn't it a pity that the early white men didn't make complete records of the Indians? But we mustn't blame them too much, for in a hundred years students will wonder why the people of today didn't make better records of what is happening now.

The Tribes and Their Country

You know that Louisiana is a state having great differences. Part of it is hilly and part of it is low and flat. There are forests in some places and grasslands in others. The Indians knew even better than we do what nature had made in Louisiana, because they had to know in order to live. We are not surprised, then, to find that each tribe lived a little differently from every other tribe. Look at the map while we visit briefly the various parts of the state to see how they were used by the Indians.

In southwestern Louisiana, a land of prairie and marsh, lived the Atakapa Indians. Hunting and fishing must have been very good. There were ducks and geese on the lakes and there were buffalo on the prairies. The name Atakapa means cannibals, people who eat human beings. We do not know for certain if they were cannibals, for their name, Atakapa, was given to them by other tribes. Some early reports say that the Atakapa didn't live in towns and didn't farm, but instead wandered over the country hunting and fishing. These reports are not true. The Atakapa did farm to some extent at least, and they did live in villages as you can see on the

[53]

map. Notice that all of their villages are located on the banks of rivers or bayous.

The part of Louisiana that lies between the Mississippi River and Bayou Teche was occupied by the Chitimacha tribes. There are many lakes, rivers, and bayous. Much of the area is swampy. It is still good for hunting and fishing. It must have been even better in the olden days, although it never had many buffalo. The Chitimacha spent a great deal of time hunting and fishing but they were good farmers too. They cleared big fields on the high ground along the streams. See on the map how their towns, too, were all on rivers or bayous.

The part of Louisiana that lies north of Lake Pontchartrain and east of the Mississippi River is called the Florida Parishes. The Muskogee tribes lived mainly in that section of the state. Much of this area is either flat land or hills covered with pine forests. Pine forests are not very good for hunting, nor do pines generally grow on good farming land. As the map shows, the Muskogee villages were either on the Mississippi River, along Pearl River, or on the shores of Lake Pontchartrain. The pine hills were visited for only one thing: to get stone for making arrowheads. The Indians camped for a few days at places where there was gravel. When they had all the stone they needed for a while, they went back to their homes on the rivers or on the lake.

The southern part of the big triangle made by the Mississippi and Red rivers was the home of the Natchez tribes of Louisiana. A large part of this area is swampy, with many lakes and streams. Hunting and fishing are good. There is plenty of the very best land for farming. Yet we know of only two tribes, the Avoyel and the Tensas, in this excellent region. The Avoyel lived on Red

[54]

River and the Tensas lived on the Mississippi. What could have been wrong with the land lying between the two rivers? Many people had lived there during the time of the mound builders. Perhaps the absence of people during later times was due to the sickness and fighting that we mentioned before. This is the part of Louisiana where DeSoto and his men stayed for a long time.

For the whole big northeastern part of Louisiana named Tunica on the map, we know of only one tribe, the Koroa. This section, too, must have been excellent country for the Indians to live in. Hunting and fishing were good. There was fine farm land. Then why were so few Indians there in 1700? Did sickness and war drive them out? We are not sure.

In the Red River section of northwestern Louisiana lived the Caddo tribes. The Caddo Indians don't seem to have had much to do with the other tribes of Louisiana. Instead they formed a union with tribes living in Arkansas and Texas. There were more buffalo in northwestern Louisiana than in other parts of the state, therefore the Caddos hunted more than they farmed. As soon as they got horses from white people, they became more and more like the hunters of the Great Plains and less and less like the farmers of the rest of Louisiana.

Now that we've finished our flying trip among the Indian tribes of the state, we can make a few statements about where they lived. Look at the map and see if you agree. The towns were always built on waterways, generally on the bigger rivers and bayous. There were few towns in the marshes and in the pine forests. The Indians lived where they could best carry on the three things that brought them their living: farming, hunting,

[55]

SPANISH HORSES

BUFFALO

and fishing. They sometimes visited other parts of the state but they didn't make their homes there.

NUMBER OF LOUISIANA INDIANS IN 1700

In the table on page 108 you will see figures that tell how many Indians there were for each of the six groups of tribes. If you add all six together, you will get a total of 13,085. Today Louisiana has over 2,000,000 people, and we believe that the state can support many more. Of course we have more and far better ways of making a living than the Indians had in 1700. But it does seem that more Indians could have lived in Louisiana, with all of them having enough to eat. The big rich country where the Tunica and Natchez tribes lived could certainly have supported more than 1,655 persons. The few Indians living in Louisiana in 1700 must mean that already they were beginning to disappear before the push of the white man.

Words to explain and remember:

independent	(ĭn dḛ pĕn′dĕnt)
cannibal	(kăn′ĭ băl)
triangle	(trĭ′ăng l)
waterway	
Caddo	(Kăd′o)
Tunica	(Tōōn′ĭ kȧ)
Natchez	
Atakapa	
Chitimacha	(Chĭt ĭ măch′ȧ)
Muskogee	(Mŭs kō′gē)
West Feliciana Parish	(Fḛ lē sĭ ăn′ȧ)
Avoyel	(Ȧ voi′ yḛl)
Tensas	(Tĕn′sô)
Koroa	(Kḛ rō′ȧ)

[56]

CHAPTER 7
How Louisiana's Indians Lived in 1700

We have found *where* the Indians lived. Now we shall see *how* they lived. Let us visit a village in the year 1700. Watch closely as Atuk and his sister Yamma work, play, eat, sleep, and do all the other things that Indian boys and girls of their tribe did. When we return from our visit, we should be able to answer questions such as these: How did the Indians dress? What games did they play? What did they eat? What kind of houses did they live in? What were their wars like?

ATUK AND YAMMA

The village where Atuk and Yamma lived stood on the shore of a lake not far from the Mississippi River in central Louisiana. The lake looked like the Mississippi. It was about as wide and it was curved, like one of the bends of the big river. But there were differences too. There was no current in the lake and its water was clear. A long time ago it had been one of the bends in the Mississippi. Then the river moved its course to the east, and left the bend behind as a lake. The shores of the lake were a very fine place indeed for building a town.

There were about 30 houses in the village. All had the same shape: square at the bottom and rounded over the top. Often Atuk had watched the men build a house. He had helped carry the heavy poles that were set in the ground and bent together at the top. He especially liked

[57]

GRASS HOUSE

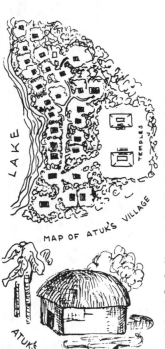
MAP OF ATUK'S VILLAGE

ATUK'S HOUSE

the plastering when the frame was covered with mud. He had learned to cover the mud plaster with palmetto leaves. Finally, he knew how to put the big cane mats over the top, and around the sides and tie them firmly together. Such a house, Atuk knew, lasted a long time. It was warm in winter and cool in summer. Atuk's father had told him about the grass houses made by the Caddo tribes who lived on Red River. He had seen palmetto houses like those used by the coast Indians. Grass and palmetto houses could be built in a short time, but they weren't as comfortable as his house, and they didn't last very long. Atuk felt a little sorry, especially on a cold winter night, for the poor people who didn't have good houses.

The 30 houses in Atuk's village were scattered up and down the high shore of the lake for about a mile. Each house stood in a clearing, or open space, connected with the next one by a path through the woods. About halfway between the two ends of the village was a bigger opening in the trees. Here the ground was smooth, level, and packed very hard. On two opposite sides of the big clearing were large rectangular buildings set on low, flat-topped mounds. The buildings were churches or temples. Sometimes the men and boys played ball and other games in the square between the temples. But it was not the proper place for children to run and shout.

Not far from the temple clearing was a house like all the others except that it was bigger. It was the home of Yamma's best friend, Nalap. Nalap's father was chief of the village, just as his own father had been. Some day Nalap's little brother would become chief, that is, if the people thought he would make a good one. Yamma liked to look at Nalap's father, for he was a big man,

[58]

and he wore a beautiful feather bonnet and carried a great long pipe to show that he was chief. Nalap's house was a grand place to play. It was so large that the children could have a part of it all to themselves.

INDIAN CHIEF

But there isn't much playing on the day we arrive at the village. It is the fall season and there are a great many things to do before winter comes. The harvest must be finished. Houses need repairs. There are fields to clear for the spring planting. There will be a fall hunting trip. Wild fruits and nuts must be gathered. A raid against the bad Indians who live on Red River is being planned.

Atuk and Yamma are helping their mother on this fine clear morning. They are out in the field that lies back of their house, gathering the last of the summer crops. Corn, sweet potatoes, pumpkins, squashes, beans, and tobacco all go into big baskets. The children bend to their loads as they follow the path to the house. Their mother drops her load in front of the door to a little building that stands high above the ground on four slick and shiny posts. This is the storehouse, made to keep out mice and squirrels. Into it go the baskets to be emptied and then returned to the field for another load.

THE STORE HOUSE

By noon the harvesting is finished. The storehouse is nearly full. Atuk would like to have the afternoon off to play, but he is told that he must help his father and their neighbors, who are clearing new fields. So Atuk carries a stone axe over his shoulder as he walks through the woods to join the men. He is set to chopping and piling brush while his father girdles trees that are too big to cut down. Girdling means to cut all the bark off to a height of about two feet. Removing the bark kills the trees. Then there will be no green leaves to keep

[59]

the sun from reaching the ground and the growing crops. In about two weeks the piled brush will be dry enough to burn. After that the field will lie idle, until it is time for spring planting.

First the ground will be broken up, a hard job with such poor hoes as the Indians have. Planting the seed is easy. Holes are made in the ground with a sharp stick. The seeds are dropped into the holes, then covered with earth. The growing plants must be hoed to keep down the weeds and grass. Most of the lighter work in the fields will be done by the women and children. The men are too busy with hunting and fishing to have much time for farming.

Atuk is glad when evening comes and his father says that it is time to go home. All eat heavily of the delicious fresh vegetables cooked by the mother. The evening is cool, so Atuk moves closer to the fire that burns just outside the door of the house. On one side of him is Yamma. On the other side is their grandfather. The old man smiles at the children as he says: "You have been good today. You have worked hard helping your father and mother. Go quickly to bed and I'll tell you a story."

Atuk and Yamma hurry eagerly to bed. There is nothing to do to get ready. Atuk wears only a small piece of skin around his waist. Yamma has on a short skirt. They don't even take their clothes off, nor do they put any other clothes on. They lie down on the mat beds that are raised a few inches above the ground by forked sticks. Grandfather squats on the earth floor between the two beds and says:

"What will it be tonight, children? Do you want to hear how the earth was made and how the great flood

[60]

came and covered everything? Or do you want to hear about West Wind?"

"No, grandfather, tell us how Blackbird got his red wings," answers Yamma.

"Yes, grandfather, please tell us about Blackbird," Atuk agrees.

"All right, young people, my story will be about Blackbird.

RED-WINGED BLACK BIRD

"Once upon a time a bad man became very angry with everybody. He wanted to destroy all the people, so he set the marshes on fire to burn them up. When the grass began burning, a little bird flew up into a tree and shouted a warning so the people could run to safety: 'Kunaxmiwica! Kunaxmiwica!' which you know means 'the water and all are going to burn.' The bad man answered the bird: 'If you do not go away I am going to kill you.' But the bird still shouted. Finally the bad man picked up a big shell and threw it at the bird, hitting its wings and making them bleed. That is how Blackbird got his red wings. After the fire had passed the bird said: 'Ah! you have done me good. I can find plenty of good things to eat now that you have burned over the ground.'

"The same fire came to a giant who had two little sisters. He put the girls inside the two parts of a big shellfish and held them high up, out of reach of the flames. 'Well,' he said, 'I have saved my two sisters anyhow.' You can still see on many shells the marks of the giant's fingers.

"When the people saw the marshes burning, they ran down and killed much game that had been driven into the open by the fire. Then they said to the man who had started the fire: 'Now that you have put fire in

[61]

MARSH FIRE

those tall weeds, deer, bears, and all kinds of animals have come out. We have killed more than we can use. You have helped us.' The bad man was more angry than ever and ran far away.

"Now you know why Blackbird has red wings and you know why he says, 'Kunaxmiwica.' Now isn't that a good story?"

Grandfather gets no answer. Both children are fast asleep.

Words to explain and remember:

clearing	(clēr′ĭng)
girdle	(gẽr′dl)
Atuk	
Yamma	(Yä′mȧ)
Nalap	(Näl′ȧp)
Kunaxmiwica	(Kōō năx mē wē′kä)

CHAPTER 8

SPRING AT THE VILLAGE

It's a warm spring day when we see Atuk and
Yamma again. We are sitting on a log that rests on the
shore of the lake. We are eager to know what Atuk and
Yamma have been doing since we saw them last fall. We
can't wait to let them tell us in their own way. We begin
asking them questions:

"Atuk, what about that big fall hunting trip? Did
you go with the men?"

"Yes, they allowed me to go with them. They knew
that I had worked extra-hard because my grandfather
was the one who taught the boys of the village how to
hunt. He showed us the right way to make blowguns
from pieces of cane. We learned to twist small pieces of
cane and to tie thistledown on one end for blowgun
darts. I practiced shooting until I could hit a squirrel
or a bird almost every time. We spent hours shooting
with our bows and arrows too. Trees and rabbits were
our targets. Only the ones who could shoot best were
allowed to go with the hunting party."

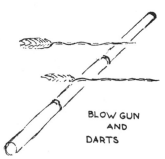

BLOW GUN
AND
DARTS

"What else did you have to do, Atuk, to prepare for
the trip?"

"We men and boys didn't have to do much except
to get our blowguns and bows and arrows in perfect
order. The women made several pairs of moccasins for
each of us. They also packed bags of corn for us to carry
as food."

RAFT

·SALT PAN

"Weren't you excited, Atuk?"

"Indeed I was excited, especially when the big day came for starting. It was the first long trip that I had ever made. There were 15 of us big boys and men who left in pirogues early one morning. For two days we paddled along the little bayou that leads out of our lake. Then we hid the pirogues in the brush and walked· toward the west. When we came to rivers that were deep or swift, we made rafts out of bundles of cane to ferry us across.

"At last we arrived one evening at a very strange place. All around was a low hill. In the center was a large clearing with a little pond. I was very thirsty and tried to drink the pond water. The old men laughed when I spit it out because it was salty. We stayed at this place for about two weeks. Other Indians had been there before us. We found some broad, shallow clay pans which they had left. Every day we put salty pond-water into the pans and set them in the sun. When the water was gone, gray salt was left in the bottom of the pans. At the end of two weeks we had filled several sacks."

"But, Atuk, what did you eat all that time? Your corn must have been gone."

"Yes, our corn was gone, but we had plenty of meat to eat. We didn't need all the men to help with the salt-making, so some of them hunted with their bows and blowguns. We had deer, squirrels, ducks, and rabbits. Three of the oldest and best hunters were gone for several days, looking for buffalo. Buffalo meat was what we really came to get."

"Couldn't you find buffalo any nearer your home, Atuk?"

[64]

"No," he replies, "not any more. Grandfather says that many years ago there were a few near our village. Now we always have to go toward the Red River to find buffalo."

"Go ahead and tell about the hunt, Atuk. We will try not to interrupt so often."

"Well, our salt-making over, we started home a different way. We were going to a place where the hunters had reported seeing buffalo. We got close to the place about noon, one day. We tied our dogs so that they wouldn't scare the big animals. We pushed quietly through the trees until we could see a large prairie spreading out before us. Sure enough, there were buffalo grazing on the heavy grass. We tried to sneak through the grass to get close enough to shoot. Suddenly the wind changed and blew our scent right to the buffalo. As soon as they smelled us, they kicked up their heels and started to run away."

"So you didn't get any buffalo, after all your hard work and long trip?"

"Oh yes, we did. As soon as the buffalo started to run we turned the dogs loose. When the dogs got close, the buffalo turned and stood facing the dogs, trying to kill them with their horns and hoofs. That was our chance. We ran in and began to shoot. I didn't kill any but my father got two. Altogether we killed six."

"But, Atuk, what could you do with so much meat? A buffalo is a very big animal. You couldn't carry all of the meat home, could you?"

"First, we and the dogs ate all that we could hold. That was a great deal of meat. Nothing in the world tastes better than buffalo ribs roasted over the fire. We cut out the tongues to carry home. Then we trimmed

[65]

the meat off the heavy bones in fairly thin chunks and slices. We hung the pieces on pole frames over a smoky fire. The smoke was to keep the flies away. After about two days in the sun the meat seemed to shrink up. It had become dry and light, so that it would keep and was easy to carry. By the time we started for the hidden pirogues with our heavy loads of dried meat, we had wasted very little of the buffalo."

"But is the dried meat good to eat?"

"Indeed it is," interrupts Yamma, "We were very glad to see the men arrive with the meat and salt. I have never had fresh buffalo meat, but I don't believe it can be any better than dried meat."

"What were you doing, Yamma, while the hunters were gone?"

"I was just as busy as Atuk. I helped my mother when she needed me and all of us girls got together during our spare time to learn about things that an Indian woman should know."

"It sounds as though both you and Atuk have to go to school."

"Of course we do. We don't have schoolhouses and books but we do have many things to learn. While Atuk and the other boys are learning to hunt and fish, to make pirogues, and how to fight, we girls are learning to cook, to make clothing, plant gardens, and to make baskets and pottery. We know that we must some day do all these things. We must also carry in the game, cut the wood and tend the fires, and look after the children."

"Stop! It sounds as though the women do all the work, Yamma."

"Yes, I suppose that it does. But the men have to do several things that I haven't mentioned yet. They

[66]

make most of the household utensils used by the women. Then too, they have to know all about our people, who they are and where they came from. They are the priests who direct the worship of our gods. They are the doctors who cure the sick. Indian women don't feel that the men do too little."

"All right, Yamma, we agree that the men are busy. But we'd like to hear more about what you did while Atuk was away."

"First we went to the woods and the lake to gather the seeds of palmettos and pond lilies. They are very good to eat, you see. Then we picked persimmons, wild beans, and wild grapes. We dug wild potatoes down by the edge of the swamp. We gathered nuts that were falling from the trees: walnuts, pecans, and hickory nuts. I'm glad that berries don't ripen in the fall or we would never have finished."

"I'm glad you worked so hard," says Atuk. "All those things tasted very good last winter."

Yamma continues: "Then we women had to make warm clothing for the cold weather. For the men there were long leggings and shirts made of two deerskins. We made cloaks for mother and me. Mother's was a net which we covered on the outside with feathers. We wove my cloak from the bark of the mulberry tree.

"I dressed skins and made moccasins. It is not hard to make moccasins. The feet are cut from a single piece of skin and sewed along two seams, one up the front and the other up the back. Then we sew on a flap that wraps around the ankle and is tied.

"I learned how to split green cane with my teeth to make baskets and how to mold clay into pots to be baked in the fire. I spent many hours in front of the upended

[67]

LEGGINGS ◉ ◉ SHIRT ◉ ◉ CLOAK ◉ ◉

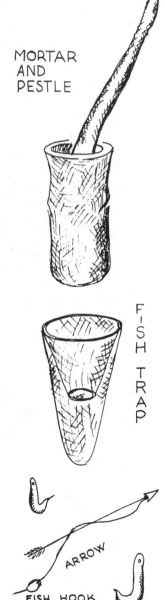

MORTAR
AND
PESTLE

FISH TRAP

ARROW

FISH HOOK

log that father had hollowed out, pounding shelled corn with a heavy pole. I sifted the flour and made corn bread."

"Yamma, do you mean to tell us that you did all those things while Atuk was gone?"

Yamma laughs heartily: "No, of course not. I've been learning and working for as long as I can remember."

We decide to give Yamma a rest and get back to Atuk.

"Atuk, you haven't said much about fishing. Don't you fish?"

Atuk is surprised. "Of course we do. We have five different ways to catch the many kinds of fish.

"Two pieces of bone tied together are our hooks. We weave nets of cedar twine. Big fish are shot with long, bone-tipped arrows. Strings and floats tied to the arrows show us where to paddle after the fish in our pirogues.

"We have a trap that is especially good for buffalo fish. Willow sticks are woven into two cones of different length. The shorter cone is left open at both ends, and is slipped into the larger one. The big ends of the two cones are bound together. Fish swim through the big opening, down the funnel, and through the small opening of the shorter one. They never seem to find their way out again.

"We have another way to fish that may sound strange to you. We use this method in pools of water where there is little current. From a root comes a poison that is stirred into the water at the head of the pool. The poison makes the fish helpless and they come to the surface where we can gather them in. The poison does not hurt the fish for eating."

[68]

"My! Atuk, with so many different things to eat, I suppose that you people never want for food."

"Not very often. Generally we have something, even if we have to eat only one thing until we get tired of it."

"Now, Atuk, we want to hear about the war. You told us last fall that your warriors were going to fight some bad people who live on Red River. Why did you want to fight with them? Did you go yourself? What happened?"

"Help! Not so many questions," begs Atuk. "Please let me tell about the war in my own way.

"We had to fight the Red River people because they had attacked our village, killed two of our people, and carried two more away as slaves.

"After we were rested from our hunting trip, our two war chiefs called a meeting of all men who were old enough to be warriors. The chiefs said that our village had been attacked because we had several times gone near Red River to hunt. They said we must defend our hunting rights. Then too, we must have revenge for our people who were killed and captured in the attack.

"The chiefs called for those who wanted to go to war. I wanted to go, but I wasn't allowed to because I had never fought before. The Red River people were good fighters and the trip to their village would be long and hard. Twenty men who had been tried in battle were selected. My father was among them. From him I learned what happened.

"The 20 warriors left their homes and moved to one of our village houses where nobody lived. For four days they stayed there. Part of the time they sang and danced.

[69]

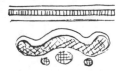

They ate no food but corn. Each warrior in turn told of his brave deeds in former wars.

"Early one morning the war party started out, walking toward the west. They carried very little food with them, only corn meal and dried meat. My father and two other men went ahead. They were scouts sent to spy on the enemy. The two war chiefs made all the warriors keep very quiet.

"For a whole week we waited anxiously for news. Finally we saw the war party returning. We ran out to meet them, to find out what had happened. I saw my father, but one of the war chiefs hadn't come back. One of the warriors was leading a strange little boy who looked very frightened. Another warrior carried the bloody scalps of two of the enemy who had been killed in the battle.

SCALPS

"Soon we heard crying and wailing from the home of the war chief who had lost his life. We knew that the women of the house were cutting their hair to show that they were in mourning. For a long time they wouldn't paint their faces nor would they appear at public gatherings. The little boy captured by our men was given to the family of the dead chief.

"The returned warriors went immediately to the house where they had stayed before going to war. There they remained for four days' more of singing and dancing. They had to do this because of the death of the war chief and because two of our men had killed and scalped two of the enemy.

"We had enough of war and killing by this time. We were glad when a messenger from a friendly village said that the Red River people were ready for peace.

Many from our town went to the friendly village. There they and the Red River people sang, danced, and smoked a pipe together. Then the war was over."

Words to explain and remember:

thistledown   (thĭs'l down)
persimmon   (pẽr sĭm'ŏn)
current   (cûr'ĕnt)
revenge   (rĕ vĕnj')
mourning   (mōrn' ing)

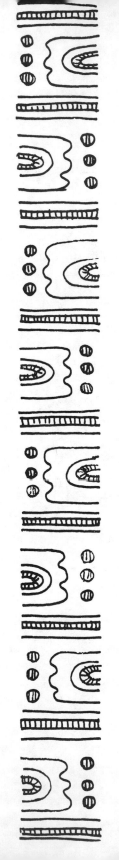

CHAPTER 9
ATUK AND YAMMA GROW UP

We sit silently on the log and think about all of the things that Atuk and Yamma have told us. We realize that we have kept our Indian friends busy answering our questions. Perhaps they have something to tell us that we haven't asked about. So we turn to them with still another question: "What else has happened since we saw you last fall?"

Atuk and Yamma look at each other and smile. "You tell them, Atuk," says Yamma.

Atuk stands up straight before us and points a finger at himself. After several minutes he turns and points at Yamma. All this time he has said not a word. Finally he asks, "Haven't you noticed something different about us?"

We have felt that their appearance is somehow changed, but we've been too busy with other matters to find out just what the difference is. When we look closely at them, they seem older and really grown up. We realize that they aren't the children of last fall.

Atuk's hair is cut short except for a few long hairs to which he has tied two feathers. On his bare chest is the figure of a snake. It looks as though it had been drawn with red, blue, and black pencils. We have seen something like it before on sailors. It is called tattooing. Not pencils, but sharp bone needles pricked the colors right into the skin. The figure of the snake will be with Atuk as long as he lives.

Yamma also is tattooed. Her hair has been cut only enough to make bangs over her forehead. The rest of her hair hangs long and straight over her shoulders. Both Atuk and Yamma wear bracelets of bone and necklaces of shell. Their ears have been pierced. Atuk has shells in his; Yamma, big plugs of baked clay.

After we have looked at them curiously for a while, Atuk explains proudly: "We were children when you saw us last. Now we are man and woman. We have become real members of our tribe. During the winter all of us who were from 13 to 15 years old were told that we were no longer children. We must learn to live and act as grown-ups.

"Yamma stayed in one corner of the house for 10 days. For three days she had nothing to eat, only water to drink. Her hair was cut in bangs over her forehead, as you see. She was shown how to paint her body with stripes of different colors.

"We boys had to run races with each other so that we would be strong. We had to walk barefoot through a fire without crying. That was to make us brave.

"I went alone to a little island that lies far back in the swamp. I lay on the ground and ate nothing. I drank but little water. Finally I became very weak. Then I had a dream. A raven appeared and told me that I must always be brave and trust in him. For the rest of my life he would help and protect me. That is why I wear these two raven feathers in my hair."

"But, Atuk, don't you believe in God? Won't He help and protect you?"

"Yes, of course I believe in our great god who is the

sun. He made the world and everything that is in it: the trees, the animals, the rocks, the rivers, and man himself. He told the people that they should be good. He told us how we must live.

"It is to honor the sun that we build temples and keep fires burning in them all the time. The priests tend the fires and tell us when and how we shall worship. Sometimes we sing and dance. Sometimes we have great feasts. At other times we fast and go without food for several days. We show that we are thankful for good crops and good hunting. We honor the sun for his part in bringing us victory in war.

"But the sun has many things to do. He is old and tired. He can't look after each one of us. That is why I have Raven to help and protect me."

"Protect you from what, Atuk? Do you mean against war and accidents?"

"Yes, war and accidents, and other things too. The sun lives far away from the earth, but there are many spirits who live all about us. They are in animals, in rocks, in trees, and in the water. Some of the spirits are good and want to help us. Others are evil and will do us harm if they can. We must know just who the spirits are and where they live. We must see that the good ones help us and that the bad ones don't hurt us."

"How can you do that, Atuk?"

"There are different ways for different spirits. We may go to the priests. Sometimes we call on our own special spirits to help us. My special spirit is Raven, you remember. We say little prayers to some spirits. To others we give offerings of food or of tools and weapons.

"Sometimes, try as we may, we can't please some evil spirit. He enters our bodies and makes us sick. We call

[75]

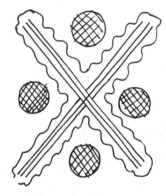

the doctor, who is generally the same person as the priest. The doctor decides what is wrong and tells us how to be cured of our illness. Some doctors cure by singing and dancing until they become very much stronger than the evil spirit. Then they command it to leave the body of the sick person. Other doctors give the patient roots to eat or wild tea to drink. They may tell him to take sweat baths. Our doctors are very good. Their patients generally get well. But sometimes every remedy fails and the sick person dies."

"What happens when someone dies, Atuk?"

"Of course the family and clan of the dead person mourn their loss. The body is buried in a low mound. Sometimes the bones are burned first and the ashes put in the grave. My father says that the Red River Indians bind dead bodies to platforms that rest on high posts or in trees. Always we put some of the things that belonged to the dead person in his grave. The spirit that has left the dead body may need them."

"Atuk, do you believe in a spirit world? Is there a heaven and a hell?"

"There are two spirit worlds, a good one and a bad one. The spirits of good people go to a place that is always fine. Hunting and fishing are good and crops grow well. The spirits of wicked people go to a place where there are swarms of mosquitoes and never much to eat. Once in a while a spirit gets back to this world by entering the body of a newly-born baby. Some spirits have lived many times in the bodies of different persons."

"You said something about a clan, Atuk. What does the word mean?"

Atuk smiles and turns to his sister: "I think that Yamma should answer that question."

Yamma is eager to tell us: "You see, our tribe is divided into five parts named after animals: wolf, bear, dog, lion, and snake. These five parts are the five clans. A father and a mother always belong to different clans. All the children, both boys and girls, are members of their mother's clan. Our father is a bear. Our mother, Atuk, and I are wolves. We three understand the wolves and they understand us because we are distantly related to each other. Mother can go into the woods and tell the wolves to go away from the village."

"But Yamma, if Atuk is a wolf, why does he have a snake tattooed on his chest? Why not a wolf?"

Yamma laughs at our ignorance as she answers, "Oh, figures tattooed on the chest have nothing to do with the clan. Atuk selected the snake only because he liked it."

We sit on the log and think dreamily of the things that we have heard. But the sun is getting low in the west. Soon we must leave Atuk and Yamma to go back to our world of today. There is time for one more question before we say goodbye. We will ask it of Yamma.

"Yamma, you and Atuk have talked most of the time about work and the things that you have to do. Don't you ever play? Don't you have any games?"

"Certainly we do. We play and we have many fine games. The boys see who is the fastest runner. They have pirogue races on the lake. They shoot at marks and they have contests to see who is the best hunter and who the best fisherman. The men and boys play a ball game together. Each player carries two bats or rackets. The two sides are chosen. Each side tries to knock the leather ball through the other's goal. It's a rough game, I can tell you, but it's fun to play and exciting to watch.

"Another sport is called the chunkey game. A pot-

BALL AND RACKETS

[77]

THREE CANES

DRUM

tery dish is rolled along the ground. While it is moving, the players throw long poles. The winner is the one who gets his pole closest to the place where the plate stops rolling.

"We girls play some of the same games that the boys play, but we have one of our own that we like better. We split a cane in half and cut off three short pieces. Then we guess how the pieces will land on the ground after they are thrown up in the air. One player guesses that the three outsides will be up. Another guesses that two outsides and one inside will be up. A third player guesses something else. That is the best game of all, I think.

"Then there are singing and dancing. We like to dance and sing at any time. We have drums and horns to make music. The best drums are clay pots or hollow cypress knees with skin stretched tightly over them. Sometimes we beat time on a piece of wood or a dry alligator skin. The horns are nothing more than pieces of cane. You probably wouldn't think much of our orchestras, but we like to sing and dance to their music."

As Yamma stops talking it is beginning to get dark. We know that our time is up. Our friends must go back to their village. We hate to say goodbye because we know that we shall never see Atuk and Yamma again. Perhaps we are sad when we realize that we have seen the last of real Indian life in Louisiana, away back in the year 1700.

A word to explain and remember:

    tattoo   (tă tōō')

CHAPTER 10

INDIANS AND WHITE MEN

After 1700 the Indians' way of living was upset by the white people who came to settle Louisiana. There were many more white men than there were Indians. The white man had better ways to fight and better ways to make a living. The Indian had to borrow the white man's ways if he wanted to live. With white men as neighbors, he could not continue to do as his people had always done. The Indian's problem was like that of a tree that stands before a great hurricane wind. If the tree bends with the wind it may have a chance to live. If it stands straight against the wind, it will be broken and destroyed. So it was with the Indians. Some tried to change to the white man's ways, but most of them could not change fast enough and completely enough to avoid being destroyed.

A few priests, preachers, and other white men felt sorry for the Indians and tried to help them as best they could. However, most white men thought of the Indians as poor animals with no rights as human beings. Louisiana was expected to provide riches for its new settlers: at first, gold and precious stones; later, furs and valuable crops.

The early white men needed the Indians' help in several ways. The Indians were the only guides through a strange new country. They were good hunters and fishermen, who could provide food for hungry Euro-

peans. They trapped animals for the furs that the Europeans wanted so much. Sometimes they were used as soldiers to fight the white man's battles against other white men or even against other Indian tribes. Indians were needed to clear the forests and plant the crops on the white man's farm.

The whites had several methods of getting what they wanted from the Indians. There were presents: beads, guns, horses, copper kettles, steel axes, pipes, and cloth. If presents weren't satisfactory, there was strong drink. Rum and whiskey would make the Indians do things that they would never do when sober. White men tried making slaves of Indians, but that was not a successful practice. They would not work well as slaves. They became sick and useless when taken away from their homes.

Some Indians resisted every effort of the white man to use them for his own gain. There was little mercy for such as these. Since they were of no use, white men thought that they should be driven away or killed.

Most Indians thought that Europeans were gods when they saw them for the first time, and they were willing and eager to please the great people who honored them with a visit. Whatever the gods did was right, even if it was different from the Indians' way. It did not take long for them to find out that Europeans were not gods, but instead, were cruel and greedy men. Then the Indians knew that they had to do something to save their very lives.

Some tribes were foolish enough or brave enough to make war against their white enemies. Sometimes they won victories. But always more white men came with their guns and horses and the Indians lost the war. Never did all the tribes of Louisiana unite to fight together for

[80]

their rights. Even had they done so and had defeated the whites at first, they would finally have lost their battle. Europeans came in a never-ending stream to the New World. They always knew more about successful warfare than the Indians did.

Even the Indians who remained friendly to white men suffered nearly as much as the ones who fought for their land. They died of white man's diseases, sometimes to the very last member of the tribe. Some left Louisiana for strange country farther west. Those who stayed in the state were driven to the poorest lands. They became few in number. Those few were sick, starved, and hopeless. It is surprising that any of them remained alive.

Every decent white American must be thoroughly ashamed of the way the Indians were treated. He should resolve to help the ones that remain.

INDIANS IN LOUISIANA TODAY

You may have heard it said that the Indians are a dying race. That is not everywhere true. In some of the Latin American countries and even in parts of western United States there are as many or more Indians than there ever were before. While only about 1,500 Indians live in Louisiana today, you may be surprised at that number. You should remember that in the year 1700 there were 13,000 or nearly nine times as many.

Most of our Louisiana Indians still live as small tribes, and in six widely separated settlements. Many are not pure Indians, but are mixed with other races. Some belong to tribes that moved to Louisiana from eastern states since 1700.

In some ways our Louisiana Indians are alike. They

[81]

INDIAN GROUPS
OF LOUISIANA
TODAY

JENA ● TOWNS (MODERN)
CHOCTAW TRIBES

SCALE OF MILES

are generally very poor and they often live on land that
no white man wants. They all dress very much as we do.
Most of them are Christians. Few live in our big towns
or cities.

In other ways they are not alike. Some are farmers; some, trappers and fishermen; some work at almost
anything to make a living. Part of them speak their old
Indian languages; others speak only French or English.
Some make the old-time baskets, bows, and blowguns,
mainly for sale to white people. Others have lost all of
the ways of their ancestors.

The largest of today's Louisiana tribes is the
Houma. Nearly a thousand of them live along the bay-
ous south of the town of Houma in Terrebonne Parish.
In 1700 the Houma lived near Angola in West Feliciana
Parish. Driven away from Angola by the Tunica tribe,

[82]

the Houma found a new home on the Mississippi near Donaldsonville. Later they fled before the white man to the marshes of Terrebonne Parish. There they have lived ever since. From time to time they were joined by members of other tribes who were seeking safety from white men.

Living in and around Lake Charles are about a half dozen Indians. They are probably all that is left in Louisiana of the once large Atakapa tribes. A few Atakapa from Louisiana live among other Indian tribes in Oklahoma.

The remaining Chitimacha, about 60 in number, live near Charenton in St. Mary Parish. Some of the women still make the famous Chitimacha baskets just as they were made hundreds of years ago. Chitimacha baskets are probably as fine as any baskets made by any Indians anywhere, at any time.

South of Marksville in Avoyelles Parish are a few Tunica, members of the tribe that long ago drove the Houma away from Angola. It is believed that the Tunica came originally from the state of Mississippi.

We know for certain that the other Indians of Louisiana who live in groups are members of tribes that moved to our state from farther east.

In Allen Parish there are about 150 Coushattas or Koasati. The Koasati are a Creek tribe who left Alabama nearly 150 years ago. After living in Louisiana for a few years, they went on west to the plains of Texas. There they joined the Comanche buffalo hunters. Before long the Koasati were homesick for the forests and streams that they missed so much on the treeless plains. They came back to Louisiana, and here they have remained to the present day.

[83]

CHITIMACHA BASKETS

Near the town of Lacombe in St. Tammany Parish and near Jena in LaSalle Parish, live a few Choctaw Indians. The Choctaw were once a great and powerful people in Mississippi and Alabama. When they were forced out of their country by the white man, a few of them settled in Louisiana.

There are other Indians in Louisiana who live among white people and not with a tribe. There are many persons in our state who are part Indian in blood. Most of them know little or nothing of Indian ways. Many important men and women of our country are very proud to be part Indian. A person who is pure Indian should be even more proud. Any one of us should be glad to have as a friend a real American Indian.

Little has been done to help the poor Indians of Louisiana. A few white friends have worked hard to improve their conditions. Within the last few years schools have been started for some of them. It is the least that we can do to see that the Indians are properly cared for. This must be done without our telling them just how they must live. They should have the means to take care of themselves, and good land that nobody can take away from them. Their health should be looked after. We should encourage them to make the old-time baskets, bows, blowguns, drums and other Indian articles, and help them to sell these articles at a fair price. Surely we who have helped so many peoples in the far places of the world, will not continue to neglect our own Indians at home.

INDIAN NAMES IN LOUISIANA

Did you ever think how few things there are in Louisiana to remind us that this was once all Indian country? It is possible to travel over much of the state and never

[84]

see a mound, midden, arrowhead, or piece of pottery. But when we look at a map of our state, we find many reminders. Some of our towns and many of our rivers, bayous, and lakes have Indian names.

On pages 109 and 110 is a list of some of the Indian names used in Louisiana. Notice how many of them are in the Choctaw language. This will seem strange because we know that the Choctaw tribes didn't even live in Louisiana. But you must remember that the early French settlers got Indian guides from the east. Most of the guides spoke Choctaw, so it is not surprising that they gave the names in their own language.

Conclusion

Nearly 2,000 years ago the first Indians reached Louisiana. They were the real pioneers and the earliest settlers of our state. There were no people before them. There were no guides to show them where and how to live. What they did, they did for themselves. What they got, they earned by their own work.

During prehistoric time the Indians spread over most of the state. They dumped out millions of clam shells into heaps that we call middens. They built burial and temple mounds. They built groups of mounds, as at Marksville and Jonesville, and surrounded them with walls and ditches. They introduced farming and they made good and beautiful pottery. They traded for minerals from far-away places. They were generally peaceful and prosperous village dwellers.

Louisiana's historic Indians continued in much the same ways as their prehistoric ancestors. They suffered as other Indians did from the coming of the white man.

[85]

It happened that the Louisiana Indians never formed a union to fight a great war against the whites. They had no warrior who became famous like Tecumseh, Pontiac, Chief Joseph, or Sitting Bull. Because the Louisiana Indians didn't fight like the Iroquois or the Sioux doesn't mean that they lacked courage. It doesn't even mean that they lacked brave warriors.

Perhaps our Indians were best at peaceful ways. We know that they were good farmers, hunters, and fishermen. They made the beautiful Chitimacha baskets. We see something in their religion that placed them above most Indians of surrounding states.

We shall always be proud of our Louisiana Indians.

Words to explain and remember:

hurricane	(hŭr' ĭ kăn)
resist	(rḕ zĭst')
ancestor	(ăn' sĕs tēr)
Terrebonne Parish	(Tĕr' bŏn)
Angola	(Ăn gō' là)
Koasati	(Kō ä sä' tē)
Comanche	(Kō măn' chē)
Lacombe	(Lä cōm')
St. Tammany Parish	(Sănt Tăm'ăn ĭ)
Choctaw	(Chŏk' tô)
Tecumseh	(Tḕ kŭm' sĭ)
Pontiac	(Pŏn' tĭ ăk)
Iroquois	(Ir' ō kwoi)
Sioux	(Sōō)

CHAPTER 11

LOUISIANA INDIAN TALES*

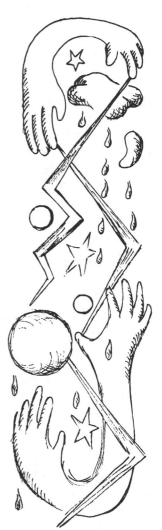

Like all people who have no writing and no books, the Indians had many legends and stories which were handed down from one generation to another. Some of the tales are about important things, such as the creation of the world, the history of the tribe, or the way in which the gods must be worshipped. Other tales were told just because the storyteller liked them and his listeners enjoyed hearing them. Indian children heard the stories over and over again until they knew them by heart. Then they could tell them to their own children and the stories would not be lost. That is the way it was all over the world before there were writing and books.

Most of the tales once told by Louisiana Indians are forgotten, but we do know many that were told by Indians who lived close to Louisiana. Here are some real Louisiana Indian tales and some from tribes who were like the Louisiana Indians:

CHITIMACHA TALES

How the Great Spirit Made the World

The Great Spirit made the world and all that is in it from his own body. He didn't look like a man, be-

---

* These and the previously related myth are adapted from the following sources: Swanton, John R., Bull. 43 and Bull. 88, Bur. of Amer. Ethn.; and Bushnell, David I., Jr., Bull. 48, B.A.E., and Amer. Anthropologist, vol. 12.

cause he had no eyes and no ears. But he could see everything and he could hear everything, and he knew everything.

First there was nothing but water, hiding the earth everywhere. The Great Spirit made fish and shellfish to live in the water. Then he told Crawfish to dive under the water and bring up mud to make the earth. As soon as Crawfish had done this, the Great Spirit made men. He called the earth and the men "Chitimacha."

The Great Spirit gave the Chitimacha laws to live by. For a while all was well in the world. Then the Chitimacha became careless and forgot the laws. The world was no longer good and men did not care to live. The Great Spirit knew that something must be done. He thought and thought and finally he made tobacco and women. These he gave to the Chitimacha.

But still, all was not well. The animals made fun of men because they had neither fur nor feathers to cover their bodies. The Chitamacha begged the Great Spirit to help them. Help them he did. He gave men bows and arrows. "Shoot the animals," he said. "Eat their flesh and use their skins to make clothing." He showed the Chitamacha how to make fire with two pieces of wood and taught them how to cook their food.

The world needed light and heat, so the Great Spirit made the moon and the sun. The moon was a man and the sun was his wife. The Great Spirit told them that they must bathe often in order to be strong enough to give off light and heat. The sun did what the Great Spirit said. She bathed often and kept herself bright and shining. The Chitamacha have always honored the sun and she has always been kind to them. Many times she has stood still so that the Chitamacha

[88]

would have time to defeat their enemies or to finish the jobs they were doing.

The moon did not obey the order of the Great Spirit. He took no baths. To this day he is pale and gives off no heat. He can still be seen chasing across the sky trying to catch the sun.

Gifts from the Great Spirit

Once 20 Chitimacha men set off toward the north until they came to the edge of the sky. While they were trying to pass under the sky, it fell upon them, killing all but six. The six men walked along on the sky floor until they came to the Great Spirit. After a long visit the Great Spirit asked them, "How are you going to get back to the earth?"

The first man said, "I'm going to turn myself into a squirrel. Watch me get down." So he turned himself into a squirrel and started out. He had gone only a short distance when he slipped and fell to the earth. That was the end of him.

The second man turned himself into a dog, and the third man into an opossum. Both were only well started when they too fell to the earth and were killed.

The fourth man wisely said, "I shall go back to the earth as a spider." "Very well," answered the Great Spirit. "I will make you a doctor. You can cure people when they are ill and keep them from dying." So the spider-man spun his thread and lowered himself to the earth. Just as he arrived, a Chitimacha who had been sick for a long time died. If the new doctor could have arrived in time, there would never have been deaths in the world.

The fifth man said he would turn himself into an eagle and fly back to the earth. The Great Spirit taught

[89]

him how to catch fish, and told him to carry the gift to the people living below.

The sixth man turned himself into a pigeon. To him the Great Spirit gave corn and told him how to plant it, how to gather it when it was ripe and how to cook it.

Many, many were the gifts of the Great Spirit. The Chitimacha never forgot to honor him for all the things he had done for them.

The Flood

A long time ago there was a great flood that covered all the earth. As the water began to rise, people wondered what they were going to do. "I know," said one, "we'll build a big clay pot and it will carry us on the water like a boat."

So everybody got busy and worked hard until the pot was done. It was finished just as the water reached the top of the hill on which they had been working. As it floated away in the deep water, only two people managed to get aboard, but as it moved under the branch of a high tree, two rattlesnakes dropped in. The people were kind and let the rattlesnakes stay. The rattlesnakes were very grateful. In the old days they always guarded the houses of the Chitimacha.

While the flood was high, the redheaded woodpecker hooked his claws in the sky and hung there. The water came up so far that it covered part of the woodpecker's tail. He still wears the muddy color on the part of his tail that was under water.

After the water had gone down some, the woodpecker was sent to find land. He came back without finding any. Then the dove was sent to find land. He came back with a single grain of sand. The grain of sand was placed on the sea and stretched out until the dry

[90]

land was all there just as it had been before. The Chitimacha still call the dove "ground-watcher."

West Wind

A little boy named Ustapu was lying in his bed close to the shore of a lake. His people had come to the lake and wanted to get to the other side. They couldn't cross because the wind was too strong, blowing big waves upon the lake.

As he lay there, Ustapu saw a boy waving a big turkey-feather fan. "Look," he said to the other Indians. "There is West Wind waving his fan and making the big wind. I can break his arm. Then the wind will fall and we can get across." The people laughed at Ustapu. "What can you do?" they asked.

The laughter made Ustapu angry. "I'll show them," he said to himself. He reached down at his feet and picked up a big shell. He threw the shell at West Wind, breaking the arm that was waving the fan. The wind stopped and the Indians got across the lake.

You can always tell which arm West Wind is using to make the wind. If the wind is strong, he is using his good arm. If the wind is gentle, he is using his broken arm.

LOUISIANA CHOCTAW TALES

How the Snakes Got Their Poison

Long ago there was a vine that grew along the edges of bayous in shallow water. The vine was very poisonous. When the Choctaw swam close to the vine they were poisoned and very often they died.

The vine liked the Choctaw and didn't want to poison them. So he called all the snakes together to see what could be done. Up to that time the snakes had no

[91]

RATTLE SNAKE

TURKEY AND TURTLE

poison. The vine explained his trouble. "What shall I do?" he asked the snakes.

The rattlesnake spoke up, "I'll take part of your poison, but before I strike, I'll give warning by rattling my tail." This he always does.

The water moccasin was next. "I'll take part of your poison, but before I strike, a Choctaw must step right on me." And the water moccasin keeps his word.

The little ground rattler was the last of the snakes to speak. "I'll take the rest of your poison, but I'll jump at a person whenever I have a chance." The ground rattler lives up to his promise.

Turtle and Turkey

Turtle met Turkey on the road one day. "Turtle, why are you hard, without any fat?"

"I was born that way," said Turtle.

"But even if you are lean you can't run very fast," answered Turkey.

"Oh, yes I can; just watch me," and poor Turtle went crawling down the road as fast as he could.

Turkey laughed and laughed as he just walked along and easily beat Turtle. How easy it was! Say! here was a chance for some fun.

"Turtle, lend me your shell for a while."

"I will, if you promise to bring it back soon," answered good-hearted Turtle.

Turkey put the shell over his head to look like a turtle, and walked down the road until he met some more turtles. "How about a race?" asked Turkey.

The turtles were willing to race. Turkey beat them easily and ran laughing away in the woods, forgetting all about the shell he had borrowed.

[92]

Raccoon and Opossum

Coon and Possum met in the woods one day. In those days Possum had a large bushy tail, but it was all white, not striped and dark like Coon's.

Possum said to Coon, "Why is your tail dark with stripes on it, while mine is only white?"

"Well, I was born that way, but I can tell you what you can do to get a tail like mine."

"I will do what you tell me, if I can have a dark striped tail like yours," said Possum.

So Coon told Possum to build a fire and hold his tail in it and that soon the white hairs would turn brown.

Possum built a fire and stuck his tail into it. But he left it there so long that the hairs were all burned off, and his tail has been bare ever since.

POSSUM AND COON

Why Possum Has a Large Mouth

It had been a dry season. There was very little food and Deer had become very thin and weak. One day he met Possum. Possum was fat and strong. "Why are you so fat when I am so lean?" asked Deer.

And Possum answered, "I live on persimmons, and they are big and fine this year."

"But how do you get persimmons which grow so high above the ground?"

"That is very easily done," replied Possum. "I go to the top of a high hill, and then I run down as fast as I can and strike a persimmon tree so hard with my head that all the ripe persimmons fall to the ground. Then I sit there and eat until I can hold no more."

"I can do that," said Deer. So he went to the top of a hill, then turned and ran down with all his power.

POSSUM AND DEER

[93]

He hit the tree so hard that he broke all his bones and died.

Possum laughed so much that he stretched his mouth and has never been able to make it small again.

The Hunter Who Became a Deer

One night a hunter killed a deer and then lay down to rest until morning. He was surprised when he awoke at sunrise to see the deer alive and to hear him speak.

"Will you go with me to my home?" asked the deer.

"Yes, I will go," said the hunter.

So the hunter dropped his bow and went with the deer. They traveled for a long time until they reached a cave where lived the king of the deer. The hunter was made welcome and was offered a place to sleep by the fire.

While the hunter was asleep, the deer fitted hoofs to his feet, horns to his head, and a skin to his body. When he awoke he looked just like a deer.

The hunter's mother searched the woods until she found her son's bow. Then she was sure that he was dead. While she was mourning, a herd of deer approached. One big deer stepped out and spoke to her in Choctaw, "Don't mourn, Mother; I am your son and I am alive."

The mother brought her deer-son to camp. She begged the men to take off his skin, horns, and hoofs, even if it killed him. "Better a dead son than a son turned to a deer," she said.

So the men took off his hoofs and horns. But when they took off his skin, the hunter began to bleed and soon he was dead. His mother mourned, but she was glad that her son was no longer a deer.

[94]

NATCHEZ TALES

The Owl and the Perch

Once the owl caught a perch in a pool that was nearly dry. The owl was about to eat the perch. The perch said, "Wait a little. Let me first sing a song for you to dance by. I am a good singer and I know some fine songs for dancing."

"Very well," said the owl, "but remember that I am going to eat you anyhow."

The perch told the owl to carry him to a good clean place where there was room to dance. The owl walked through the woods until he came to a clear bank by a big pool of water.

"This is the place," said the perch. "Put me on the bank, then dance back and forth four times. The fourth time you can eat me."

The owl began to dance. Three times he danced along the bank, but as he turned for the fourth time, the perch flopped off the bank into the pool of water. So the perch fooled the owl and the owl lost his dinner.

The Turtle

A turtle came out of the water to sun himself on a log. For a while the sun was bright and warm. Then a big cloud came up and the turtle saw that it was going to rain. The turtle said to himself, "My! my! it's going to rain. I'll get wet!" So he slid off the log back into the water.

Story of a Buffalo

Once a hunter was overtaken by darkness and thought, "I will camp for the night and go home to-morrow morning."

Nearby was something that looked like the roots of an overturned tree. "I will make my fire here," decided the hunter.

So he hung his bow on the roots and built his fire. Soon up jumped the roots and ran away, carrying the hunter's bow with them. Then the hunter saw that it was a buffalo and not a tree at all.

The Mosquito

A Natchez was out hunting one time when he heard a noise coming from a long way behind him. "Wamp, wamp, wamp," it went.

"It must be someone after me," thought the man, and he began to run through the woods.

Soon he heard a rushing noise close behind him. He turned to see a giant mosquito heading directly for him. The frightened hunter jumped behind a tree. The mosquito turned toward the tree, striking it so hard that his bill ran all the way through and came out near where the Natchez was standing. The hunter pulled out his hatchet and pounded the mosquito's bill down so that he could not pull it out. Then the mosquito brought his wings forward to try to pull his bill loose. The hunter cut the wings off and put them in his pack.

"They'll make good fans for the old men," he said.

KOASATI TALES

Sickness

It was decided that there should be no sickness in the world, so all the sickness was gathered up and put into a bottle. Then the people looked for someone who could carry the bottle far up into the sky and leave it.

"I can do it," said Snipe. Up he flew, out of sight.

[96]

When he came back, he told the people that he had been to the sky. They believed him.

So the bottle was given to Snipe and he flew away. Pretty soon he was back, still carrying the bottle. While he was holding the bottle, it fell and broke into many pieces. That is how sickness was spread all over the world.

The Man and the Deer-Children

Once a hunter ran across some deer. "Don't shoot us," they begged, "and we will go home with you and and be your children. But there is one thing," they warned, "you must never tell anyone that we are deer."

So the children went home with the hunter. They wore beautiful clothes and everyone admired them. "Where did you get those fine children?" the hunter's friends wanted to know, but the hunter was silent.

Finally he was asked so many times that he answered, "They are deer-children."

Then the children made noises like frightened deer and ran away into the woods. The hunter was very sorry.

The Angry Owls

An old man told a Natchez hunter that if he swallowed a crawfish and hooted like an owl, real owls would come and bite him, pull his hair all out, and put out his fire.

The young man did not believe the story, so he swallowed a crawfish and hooted like an owl. There was a rushing of wings and a whole flock of owls came toward him. They wet their feathers, shook them over the hunter's fire, and put it out. Then the owls flew at the hunter, bit him, and pulled out his hair.

[97]

The Conceited Wren

Wren stood under a log that was close to the ground and said, "Would you not say that I am very tall? When I rise on my toes I strike my head against the sky."

Rabbit and the Ducks

Once when Rabbit was traveling through the woods he came to several ducks swimming on a pond. With a cord made fast to his waist, Rabbit dived under the ducks and tied all their feet together. When he had finished, Rabbit came up in the middle of the ducks. The ducks were frightened and flew away, carrying Rabbit with them.

Rabbit's grandmother had been making a pot and had just set it down when the ducks flew over her head. Rabbit called to his grandmother, begging her to help him down.

Grandmother picked up the pot and threw it among the ducks. The pot broke the string and Rabbit fell down at his grandmother's feet.

Rabbit Fools Wildcat

One time Rabbit came across a deer lying asleep. By and by Wildcat came along.

"See what I have killed," said Rabbit. When I have skinned it, you can help me eat it."

Wildcat was very willing to help eat the deer. As he sat waiting, Rabbit told him, "You sneak up and sit on the deer."

As soon as Wildcat sat on the deer, it woke up and began to run, with Wildcat sticking to its back.

SUGGESTIVE QUESTIONS
AND ACTIVITIES

CHAPTER 1

1. Begin a collection of things such as arrowheads and potsherds that were made and used by Louisiana Indians.
2. On a map of Louisiana find Houma, Charenton, Elton, and Jena. Name the parishes in which these towns are located. Point out Grand Lake in Cameron Parish.
3. If you live near Houma, Charenton, Elton or Jena, invite one of the Indians in your community to talk to your class about his people and their ways.
4. Draw a rectangle three inches long and two inches wide. What is the difference between a rectangle and a square?
5. Draw a pyramid.
6. If you live near an Indian mound or have seen one in another part of the state, describe it to your class.
7. Describe the work of an archaeologist in the following order:
   Getting ready to dig a mound
   Digging the mound
   Handling the specimens
   Studying the specimens
   What the archaeologist learns
8. Make a list of things in our present dump heaps or "middens".
9. If you live in or near New Orleans, Baton Rouge, Natchitoches, or Shreveport, try to make arrangements for your class to see the Indian collections at the following places:
   The State Museum, New Orleans
   The Geology School, Louisiana State University, Baton Rouge
   Northwestern State College, Natchitoches
   State Exhibit Building, Fair Grounds, Shreveport
   Dodd College, Shreveport

CHAPTER 2

1. On a map locate the following:
    Siberia
    East Cape
    Alaska
    Cape Prince of Wales
    Bering Strait
    Yukon River in Alaska
    Canada
    Great Plains in United States
    Mexico
    Central America
    South America
    Peru
2. The two little islands near the middle of Bering Strait are called Big Diomede and Little Diomede. The former belongs to Russia and the latter to the United States. They are shown only as dots on the map in your geography book. See if you can find them.
3. Draw an Indian harpooning a seal. (Save any drawings, or other things you make, for an exhibit to be held when you have finished studying "*The Indians of Louisiana*").
4. Make the following articles:
    bone punch
    bone knife
    wooden club
5. Try to start a fire as the Indians did.
6. Trace what seems to be the easiest route from Alaska all the way down to Peru. Remember to avoid high mountains if possible.
7. On your sand table make a midden village. Make your Indians of clay, let them dry in the sun, and have your mother bake them in her oven. Try to show the following things:
    houses

    midden
    baskets
    stone boiling
    making a pirogue
    making bone punches

8. If you have no sand table, make a drawing of a midden village without looking at the picture in your book.

9. Dramatize the part of the chapter you like best.

CHAPTER 3

1. On a map point out the following:
    Some of the larger bayous and rivers in Louisiana
    Arkansas
    Mexico
    The Mississippi Valley
    Lake Superior
    Marksville, Avoyelles Parish

2. Collect clay of as many colors as you can find. Moisten it and roll it between your hands into long rods; coil the rods around to make pots of different shapes; smooth your pots; let them dry in the sun; then ask your mothers to bake them. Save these and everything else you make for your exhibit.

3. Select a green tree branch for a bow. (A hickory branch is one of the best.) Peel the bark off and rub the stick with oil to "season" it and keep it from warping. Put it away to dry. Make a bowstring of tough fiber of some sort and attach it to your bow.

4. Show your class how the Indians drilled holes in rock with a piece of cane.

5. Make an Indian hoe and a shovel.

6. Write a class play about the return of Alla's father and brothers from their trip. Use as your characters Alla's father and two brothers, Alla's mother, his sister and baby brother and Alla him

self. Your play should be nearly all conversation. When you are
satisfied with it, select the characters from your class and act out
the play.

7. Build a burial mound on your sand table.
8. Make the following, if you can:
    clay pipes
    stone axes
    stone drills
9. Draw Alla's home. Be sure to show the following things in your
   picture:
    The strange traders and their wares
    The pot over an open fire
    Alla's little brother
    The corn gardens
10. Illustrate the scene you like best in this chapter.
    Explain your picture to your class.

CHAPTER 4

1. Locate Jonesville, Catahoula Parish, on the map.
2. On your sand table make several temple mounds placed around
   a plaza.
3. If you live near Jonesville, visit the remains of the temple mounds
   there if possible.
4. Make a stockade village on your sand table or draw one.
5. Make a list of things used by the Temple Mound Indians which
   earlier Indians did not have.
6. Illustrate the following sentences:
    "In their ceremonies the Indians wore masks and charms, had
     a special dress."
    "They must have revenge on the wicked neighbors who had
     brought sickness and death."

[102]

7. Explain the outline on the prehistoric Indians of Louisiana to your class. You should begin with the end of the outline, since it describes the earliest Indians.

CHAPTER 5

1. On a map point out the following:
   Cuba
   Labrador
   San Salvador Island
   East Indies
   Mexico
   Peru
   New England
   Virginia
   St. Lawrence River
   Mobile, Alabama
2. Make up signs for some words. Ask your class to guess what you are "saying."
3. Write to the Indian Bureau, Department of the Interior, Washington, D.C., and ask for the following:
   A list of materials on Indians for use in schools.
   Addresses of schools on Indian reservations with which you may correspond.
   Information about the work of the Indian Bureau.
4. Find out, if you can, other plants that we got from the Indians besides those mentioned in the text. Make posters showing as many of them as you can.

CHAPTER 6

1. Study carefully the map on page 52. Point out the sections of the state where each language group lived.

2. Turn to the table on page 108, and locate on a map of Louisiana each of the towns, rivers, lakes and bayous mentioned under the heading "Where They Lived."
3. How many tribes belonged to each language group? Which was the largest group? Which was the smallest group?
4. Suppose there were six different languages spoken in Louisiana today. What are some of the difficulties we would have?
5. What are the two main languages spoken in Louisiana today?

CHAPTER 7

1. A lake like the one near which Atuk and Yamma lived is sometimes called "Old River" or "False River." On a large map of Louisiana, see how many of these lakes you can find near the Mississippi River.
2. On the map of Atuk's village, on page 58, point out the various houses, and tell what each is.
3. On your sand table, make Atuk's home. Make some mat beds to put into Atuk's house.
4. Illustrate the scene in which Atuk and Yamma help their mother to gather the last of the summer crops.
5. Write a paper describing the clearing of fields and the planting of corn.
6. Write and act a play about the story Atuk's grandfather told.

CHAPTER 8

1. Make the following things for your exhibit:
   A blowgun and darts
   A small raft
   Some shallow salt pans
   Bone fishhooks

Arrows with floats

A fish trap

2. Bring to class some palmetto plants with berries on them.
3. Draw a picture of Yamma's mother's cloak.
4. Illustrate this sentence: "There they and the Red River people sang, danced, and smoked a pipe together."

CHAPTER 9

1. Model Atuk and Yamma in clay. When dry, use water colors for the tattooing.
2. Dramatize Atuk's dream.
3. Would it be correct to say that the Indians were "nature worshipers"? Explain your answer.
4. What is the difference between tennis and the Indian game played with a ball and rackets?
5. Play the chunkey game and the girls' split cane game.
6. Make an Indian drum.

CHAPTER 10

1. In what ways did the early white men need the Indians?
2. Divide your class into two groups. Ask one group to write papers about the white men's treatment of the Indians. Ask the second group to write papers about what we should do for our present Indians.
3. Write a letter to the State Department of Education, Baton Rouge, La., asking what is being done to educate the Indians of Louisiana.
4. There is an Indian school at Charenton, Louisiana, which is operated by the Federal government. It is called "Chitimacha School". Two or three times a week an Indian woman goes to the school to teach the girls how to make Chitimacha baskets. The boys and girls do other things in their school that might interest

you. Write and ask them to tell you about their school work. Address your letter to Chitimacha School, Charenton, Louisiana.

5. Write some poems about Louisiana Indians.

6. When you have finished your study of *"The Indians of Louisiana"* and have completed your exhibit, plan a program to be given for your parents or for some other class in your school. The following are some of the things you may plan to do:

Select members of your class to tell different parts of the story. (Be sure to have a map on which the speaker can point out the places he mentions.) At the end of each talk, another boy or girl might point out and explain the part of your exhibit that illustrates the talk. Act out one of the plays you have written or one of the Indian legends.

Select the best papers written by the class and read one or two of them. Read several of your best poems. Invite your guests to stay after the program to examine your exhibit while members of your class explain it to them. If you decide to serve refreshments, it would be appropriate to include in your menu only foods which we got from the Indians; for instance, you might serve tapioca pudding, salted peanuts and hot chocolate.

HOW TO PRONOUNCE WORDS

ā as in (a)te, p(a)le, v(ei)l
â as in f(a)re, th(e)re
ă as in c(a)t, m(a)rry
à as in (a)sk, comm(a)nd, sof(a)
ä as in c(a)lm, f(a)r, f(a)ther
å as in loc(a)l, (a)pply
ē as in (e)ven, m(ee)t, k(e)y, mach(i)ne
ė as in (e)leven, (e)vent
ĕ as in (e)dge, (e)nd
é as in pres(e)nt, rec(e)nt
ē as in writ(e)r, alt(a)r, act(o)r
ī as in f(i)ne, del(igh)t, (eye), fl(y)
ĭ as in s(i)t, lovel(y), lad(ie)s
ō as in h(o)pe, bl(o)w, s(ew), th(ough)
ȯ as in p(o)tato, (o)bey, c(o)nnect
ô as in c(o)rd, c(a)ll, l(aw), d(o)g
ŏ as in h(o)t, wh(a)t
ó as in c(o)nnect, c(o)mpare
ū as in c(u)re, (u)nit, y(ou), f(ew)
ů as in (u)nite
û as in b(u)rn, f(u)r, l(ea)rn, w(o)rd
ŭ as in c(u)t, h(o)ney, en(ou)gh
ŭ as in s(u)cceed, s(u)pport
ōō as in b(oo)t, d(o), r(u)le, thr(ew)
ŏŏ as in f(oo)t, p(u)t, c(ou)ld
ou as in h(ow), ab(ou)t, b(ough)
oi as in b(oi)l, b(oy)
g as in (g)et, (g)old
j as in (j)oy, (g)entleman, a(g)e
y as in (y)et, (y)ear
ng as in so(ng), bri(ng), fi(ng)er
ch as in (ch)in, cat(ch), ques(ti)on
sh as in (sh)ow, (s)ure, o(ce)an, na(ti)on
th as in (th)in, ba(th)
th as in (th)en, ba(the), ei(th)er
hw as in (wh)en, (wh)y
zh as in mea(s)ure, divi(si)on, Baton Rou(ge)
b, d, f, h, k, l, m, n, p, r, s, t, v, w, z are used to stand
    for their own ordinary sounds
qu—kw as in (qu)ite, (qu)ick
c—k as in (c)at or s as in (c)ity

APPENDIX 1
The Tribes of 1700

Language		Tribes	Where They Lived
Atakapa	2,455	Atakapa	1. Calcasieu River
		Atakapa	2. Mermentau River
		Atakapa	3. Vermilion River
		Opelousa	Near Opelousas
Chitimacha	3,090	Chitimacha	1. Lower Bayou Teche
		Chitimacha	2. Bayou Grosse Tete-Grand River
		Chitimacha	3. Upper Bayou Lafourche
		Washa	Middle Bayou Lafourche and Lower Mississippi River
		Chawasha	Same general location as Washa
Caddo	2,500	Kadohadacho	Near Shreveport
		Natchitoches	Near Natchitoches
		Yatasi	Near Coushatta
		Adai	Near Robeline
		Doustiony	Near Campti
		Washita	Near Columbia
Tunica	500	Koroa	Near Winnsboro (?)
Natchez	1,155	Tensas	Lake St. Joseph
		Avoyel	1. Near Marksville
		Avoyel	2. Near Alexandria
Muskogee	3,385	Houma	Near Angola
		Okelousa	Upper Atchafalaya (?)
		Bayougoula	Bayou Goula
		Quinipissa	Near Hahnville
		Tangipahoa	Both sides Lake Pontchartrain
		Acolapissa	Lower Pearl River

APPENDIX 2

Indian Names in Louisiana*

Name	Language	Meaning in English
Atchafalaya (Chăf à lĭ′ à)	Choctaw	Hacha or *river*, plus falaia or *long*; so, *Long River*
Avoyelles (Ă voi′ yĕlz)	Natchezan	*Flint People*
Bayou Funny (Bī′ōō Fŭn′ĭ Lōō′ē) Louis	Choctaw	Bayou or bayuk is *river*; Funny or fani is *squirrel*; and Louis or lusa is *black*; so, *Black Squirrel River or Bayou*
Bayou Goula (Bī′ōō gōō′là)	Choctaw	Bayou, plus goula or okla (*people*); so, *Bayou or River People*
Bogalusa (Bōg à lōō′sà)	Choctaw	Bog or *creek*, plus lusa or *black*; so, *Black Creek*
Bogue Chitto (Bōg Chĭt′tŏ)	Choctaw	Bog, plus chito or *big*; so, *Big Creek*
Caddo (Kăd′ō)	Caddo	Kado or *Chief*; *Principal*
Calcasieu (Kăl′kà shōō)	Atakapa	Katkosh or *eagle*, plus yok or *to cry*; so, *Crying Eagle*
Catahoula (Kăt à hōō′là)	Choctaw	Okhata or *lake*, plus hullo or *beloved*; so, *Beloved Lake*
Chacahoula (Chăk à hōō′là)	Choctaw	Chuka or *home*, plus hullo or *beloved*; so, *Beloved Home*
Choupique (Shōō′ pĭk)	Choctaw	The *chopique* or *mudfish* or grinnel
Coochie (Kōō′ chĭ)	Creek	Ui or *water*, plus lako or *great*, plus uchi or *little*; so, *Little Great Water*
Coushatta (Kōō shăt′à)	Choctaw	Kusha or *reed-brake*, plus hata or *white*; so, *White Reed Brake*
Houma (Hōō′mà)	Choctaw	Humma or *red*
Istrouma (Is trōō′ mà)	Choctaw	Iti or *stick*, plus humma or *red*; so, *Red Stick or Baton Rouge*

* Adapted from "Louisiana Place Names of Indian Origin" by William A. Read.

Place	Language	Meaning
Kisatchie (Kĭ săch' ĭ)	Choctaw	Kusha or *reed-brake*, plus hacha or *river*; so, *Reed Brake River*
Manchac (Măn' shăk)	Choctaw	Imashaka or *rear*, or *rear entrance*
Mermentau (Mĕr' mĕn tô)	Atakapa	Inmanatu-a, name of Atakapa chief
Mississippi	Algonquian	Misi or *great*, plus sipi or *water*; so, *Great Water*
Opelousas (Op ĕ lōō' săs)	Choctaw	Either aba (*hair*) or api (*leggings* or *legs*); so, *Black Hair* or *Black Leggings* or *Legs*
Plaquemine (Plăk' ĕ mĭn) and Plaquemines	Illinois	Piakimin or *Persimmon*
Ponchatoula (Pŏn chà tōō' là)	Choctaw	Pashi or *hair*, plus itula or *to hang*; so, *Hanging Hair* or *Spanish moss*
Shongaloo (Shŏng' à lōō)	Choctaw	Shakolo or *Cypress Tree*
Tallulah (Tà lōō' là)	Cherokee	Meaning not known
Tangipahoa (Tăn jĭ pà hō')	Choctaw	Tanchapi or *cornstalk*, plus ayua or *gather*, so, *Cornstalk Gatherers*
Tchefuncta (Chĕ fŭnk' tà)	Choctaw	Hachofakti or *Chinquapin*
Tchoupitoulas (Chŏp ĭ tōō' làs)	Choctaw(?)	Tiak or *pine*, plus foha or *rest*; so, *Pine Rest*
Tunica (Tōōn' ĭ cà)	Tunica	Ta or *the*, plus uni or *people*, plus ka; so, *The People*
Whiskey Chitto (Whĭs' kē Chĭt'tô) (Creek)	Choctaw	Uski or *cane*, plus chito or *large*; so, *Big Cane Creek*